Leader Effectiveness Training
L.E.T.

The Foundation for
Participative Management
and Employee Involvement

Dr. Thomas Gordon

G. P. Putnam's Sons • New York

To those leaders who gave me opportunity to develop new ideas within their organizations.

To the members of my organization who have endured my own continuing growth as a leader.

To my wife, Linda, and my daughters, Judy and Michele, who educate me.

G. P. Putnam's Sons
Publishers Since 1838
a member of Penguin Putnam Inc.
200 Madison Avenue
New York, NY 10016

Library of Congress Cataloging in Publication Data

Gordon, Thomas, date.
  Leader effectiveness training, L.E.T.

  Reprint. Originally published: New York: Wyden Books,
© 1977.
  Bibliography: p. 270
  Includes index.
  1. Leadership. 2. Executive ability. 3. Organizational
behavior. I. Title. II. Title: Leader effectiveness
training, LET.
  BF637.L4G63   1983   158'.4   83-11123
  ISBN 0-399-14357-2

10 9 8 7 6 5 4 3 2

This book is printed on acid-free paper. ∞

Contents

FOREWORD

This book, originally published in 1977, is still relevant to the quality of leadership in organizations. In fact, it is even more relevant in view of the unmistakable current trend away from the traditional "dominator" model of leadership toward a "partnership model," away from an emphasis on "ranking" people toward "linking" them.

Nowhere is the trend toward partnership relations more widespread than in the workplace. The traditional organizational hierarchy called for leaders to command from the top, using rigid controls and hoarding information. Today, this autocratic, top-down, command, control, and compartmentalize model of leadership is being replaced by "workplace democracy" with a radical change in managers' leadership style. Much of the problem-solving that produces products and customer service is being done by teams—some of them leaderless.

We are seeing the same trend in other important relationships, both in our own country and in many others. Women have struggled for and earned a more reciprocal, equalitarian relationship with men—in marriage as well as in the workplace. Likewise, parents who have been strongly influenced by the parent training movement are discarding the "command and obey," father-knows-best model of parenting in favor of a non-authoritarian, non-hierarchical, non-punitive model. More and more parents are beginning to understand the damaging effects of authoritarian parenting on both their children and their relationship with them. They are also learning that permissive parenting is certainly not the alternative—both parent and child must feel their needs are being met.

The trend toward democratic relationships is beginning to be observable in our educational institutions, which traditionally have hung on to a strong "dominator model" of relationships—between administrators and teachers, teachers and students, and even teachers and parents. Teachers are no longer permitted to use strong enough punishments to enforce their domination in the classroom. My own organization has played a major role in training teachers how to achieve the full participation of their students in setting classroom rules. Also, cooperative student learning teams are now widely used by teachers, and many research studies have shown the benefits of this leaderless student learning model.

In chapter II of this book I stress the wisdom of the group and encourage managers to marshal the creative resources of their group members. "Most leaders greatly underestimate the wealth of knowledge, ideas, and ingenuity lying untapped in the heads of workers." Later, I provide seven answers to the question "Why build a team?" I also stress the paradox that effective leaders act very much like group members and effective group members act like group leaders. In a recent article (November 1995) in *American Psychologist*, Dr. Wayne Cascio, of the Graduate School of Business at the University of Colorado, confirms that in many organizations today one finds that "workers are acting more like managers and managers more like workers." He goes on to document that "the managerial roles of controllers, planners, and inspectors are being replaced by coaches, facilitators and mentors."

In this book the reader will also find one full chapter devoted to empowering workers by helping them find their own solutions to problems. I wrote in 1977 that "leaders who empower their workers to solve their own problems are making a sound investment that will pay off with many benefits . . . [the workers] will become less dependent on their leaders, more self-directed, more self-sufficient, and more capable of solving their problems on their own" (p. 63). These important benefits, however, will not occur in organizations unless leaders learn the interpersonal skills needed to empower group members. This book not only acknowledges this fact but specifies what those essential skills are. And then it teaches readers how and when to use them. Today, as we are experiencing a dramatic revolution in the workplace, the critical importance of those skills is even more widely recognized.

Literally hundreds of articles and books have confirmed the need for the new breed of leaders to be trained in the interpersonal skills specified in this book, such as:

- Developing and leading participative group meetings (chapter VII)
- Practicing empathic Active Listening (chapters IV and V)
- Using non-threatening confrontation, a non-power way to influence others to change unacceptable behavior (chapter VI)
- Resolving conflicts so neither person loses and both get their needs met (chapters IX and X)
- Recognizing and avoiding the Roadblocks in person-to-person communication (chapter IV)
- Using a non-threatening alternative to performance evaluation (chapter XI)

- Selecting the appropriate kind of group meeting (chapter VII)

Since the 1977 publication of *L.E.T.*, the organization that I founded—originally known as Effectiveness Training Incorporated but recently renamed Gordon Training International—has provided leadership training to managers and supervisors in hundreds of organizations in the U.S. and in a dozen foreign countries. This book has been the textbook for that L.E.T. course, which varies in length from three to five full days. Course participants are given ample opportunity to practice communication skills and conflict-resolution procedure by role-playing and receiving coaching in the class.

Participants in the L.E.T. course consistently report that the principal value of their training was learning the necessary skills that other training experiences had failed to provide them. They complain that they have been told in the past by consultants and book authors *what* they should be doing—such as quality circles, worker empowerment, TQM, distributing leadership functions, valuing diversity, and other initiatives from top management. Seldom have they been taught *how* they can do them. However, L.E.T. provides them with the specific communication skills and problem-solving procedures they need to make such programs work.

When this book was published in 1977, it was often described as "soft," too "employee-centered." Critics were skeptical about managers holding so many group meetings and "sharing their authority" with their group members. L.E.T. was seen as a totally different paradigm of leadership, which many critics felt put too much faith in the "wisdom of the group," "employee self-motivation," "distributing leadership functions to group members." Even L.E.T.'s emphasis on using Active Listening was frequently viewed as bringing psychotherapy and "touchy-feely" behaviors into the workplace. L.E.T. was also criticized for stressing employee "happiness" and for putting too much faith in employee participation in problem-solving and personal goal setting.

However, twenty years later, we are experiencing a major transformation in organizations and the role of their leaders. It is now widely accepted that the key to leaders' effectiveness is their capability in building a competent team and working in partnership with managers and workers in other departments of their organization.

Research has shown that one of the primary reasons leaders fail is that they are promoted into positions that make it necessary to work closely with others. Being untrained in the requisite skills for building good relationships and group-centered teams, they are unable to harness the creativity of team members. They fail because they do not know how to build equalitarian or partnership relationships.

The reader of this book will learn specific skills for building such relationships. And because these skills are universal for building all kinds of collaborative and equalitarian relationships, you can use them both to strengthen your marriage and to become a more effective parent.

Unfortunately, as critically important as "relationships training" has become, a large percentage of workers never receive any training to become effective team members. In fact, many companies spend nothing at all on such training. To survive, many organizations now will need to train both leaders and employees in the skills they need to work cooperatively in partnership relationships. Companies will need to become "learning organizations."

The father of quality circles in Japan, Kaoru Ishikawa, wrote: "In management, the first concern of the company is the happiness of people connected with it. If the people do not feel happy and cannot be made happy, that company does not deserve to exist" (Ishikawa 1985). Readers of this book who learn the skills needed to make participative and democratic leadership work will be amply rewarded by the positive effects on the workers, as found in a study of fifty companies that had adapted "participative management":

"Absenteeism and turnover can be cut in half . . . people feel better about themselves. They like to go to work. They have more self-esteem and self-confidence. They have gained control over their lives, if only a little, and lost some of their sense of powerlessness" (Simmons and Mares 1983).

Dr. Thomas Gordon
Founder
Gordon Training International

Ishikawa, Kaoru. 1985. *What Is Total Quality Control? The Japanese Way*. Englewood Cliffs, NJ: Prentice-Hall.

Simmons, John, and William Mares. 1983. *Working Together: Employee Participation in Action*. New York: Alfred A. Knopf.

I. HOW YOU CAN BECOME AN EFFECTIVE LEADER

THE word "leadership," I am told, did not appear in the English language until around the year 1800. Then it took another 100 years before social scientists undertook serious study of the phenomenon of leadership. But in the last 40 years researchers have been hard at work making up for lost time, inquiring into how people become leaders, how they retain positions of leadership, how they acquire followers, how they affect group performance, and what makes for leader effectiveness. A recent comprehensive survey and review of leadership research contains a bibliography of over 3000 studies, consuming 150 pages! Obviously leadership has been intensely investigated.

Now that much of the mystery has been taken out of the concept of leadership, it is possible to describe rather precisely what it takes to be an effective leader. The thousands of studies enable us to build a model of leader effectiveness based on solid research evidence from many types of organizations and groups.

It is one of the purposes of this book to bring that model

out of the privacy of university laboratories into the public domain, where it will be easily accessible to the countless people who find themselves in positions of leadership —in government, in business and industrial organizations, in agencies and institutions, in community organizations, in schools, in families. It is time to let the public know what effective leadership is all about, so that people in all walks of life may have a criterion for judging both themselves as leaders and those who become (or offer to become) their leaders.

For today, quite unlike society in centuries past, most people live much of their lives in groups—when they work, when they worship, when they play, when they learn. And it seems all groups do need leaders, for better or for worse. But leaders can make or break a group. Their attitudes and behavior strongly influence the group's performance and also the amount of satisfaction enjoyed by group members, as everyone knows from direct experience with teachers, administrators, supervisors, committee chairpersons, coaches, managers, clergy, and elected officials.

It is equally true of our society, and a fact often overlooked, that most people at one time or another are thrust into a position of leading a group. Most people become parents, for example, a leadership position in relation to the children. The teacher, too, is a leader (of his or her classroom of students). Each person is a leader who gets chosen to direct a committee or task group, who is elected president of a volunteer organization, who assumes responsibility as a scout leader or camp director.

Of the countless people who take on these varied leadership roles, how many find it a truly rewarding and fulfilling experience? How many can honestly assess their performance as a "job well done"? How many encounter troublesome resistance to their conscientious attempts to lead—or even hostility, jealousy, unfriendliness? How many end up saying, "Never again!"?

If being a leader turns out to be a bad experience, it is almost always because of the leader's own ineffectiveness. And considering that few people ever get any kind of specific training in leader effectiveness, it is easy to understand why being a leader so often is difficult, draining, and disappointing.

A second purpose of this book, then, is to show leaders what special skills and methods they must learn to use today's "model" of effective leadership. Just understanding the model is not enough; leaders must acquire the skills to implement the model.

Take the important concept of "mutual need satisfaction," more fully explained in Chapter III. Research has shown that effective leaders are those whose group members feel their needs are getting satisfied and the leaders themselves feel they are getting their own needs met: what some call an "equitable social exchange." But how does a leader accomplish this? What specifically must a leader do to achieve this desirable state of mutual need satisfaction? You will not find the answer to those "how-to" questions in most books on leadership. Yet specific methods do exist for resolving conflicts of needs and achieving this necessary "equitable balance of benefits," the most important being our No-lose Method, explained and illustrated in Chapters IX and X. This six-step conflict-resolution method enables leaders to translate theory into practice, to make *actual* what research tells us is *ideal*.

Research findings also consistently validate the "principle of participation"—i.e., group members more readily accept new ideas and new work methods when they are given the opportunity to participate in making the decision to change and to participate in deciding how to implement the change. While you will find "employee participation" advocated in most books on leadership as an *ideal* for effective leadership, few spell out exactly how leaders can do this effectively. In Chapter VII, I break down the *abstraction* of "participative management," showing leaders how they can use varying degrees of group member participation; and I describe specific types of group meetings they can use to foster participation.

This obviously is a book of skills and methods: how to listen so that group members will talk about their problems; how to talk so that group members will be considerate of your special needs; how to conduct efficient meetings; how to identify problems and work efficiently toward good solutions; how to handle infractions of rules; how to get group members to set performance goals; how to take the threat out of performance evaluation.

Some of these skills and methods I developed myself as I worked collaboratively on practical problems with leaders in the organizations in which I served as a human relations consultant. Others (primarily the communications skills) I have borrowed from those who trained me to become a professional "helping agent" and from colleagues with whom I worked as a practicing clinical psychologist. Over the years my confidence in these skills has progressively increased—I know they work. And I know they can be taught to most leaders, a conviction based on over two decades of training several thousand leaders in my L.E.T. course, many thousands of teachers and principals in my T.E.T. (Teacher Effectiveness Training) course, and perhaps a quarter of a million parents (family leaders) in my P.E.T. (Parent Effectiveness Training) course.

These skills and methods have a greater impact on organizations when all levels of management receive the L.E.T. training. Yet it is clear that their effects can be felt in an organization when only one leader acquires the skills and methods. This was brought out in a study conducted by the Industrial Relations Center of the University of Chicago. It was a follow-up evaluation of a single leader, a plant manager, who had been taught the L.E.T. skills described in this book.

One year after this person had changed his leadership style and assumed the position of plant manager, in-depth interviews were conducted with his group members (11 foremen) and the top total management group (12 in all). Out of their 160 separate statements describing the plant manager, only five could be interpreted as suggesting undesirable characteristics. The most frequently mentioned characteristics of this leader were:

Listens with understanding; willing to discuss problems; open to ideas; gives time to listen (27 comments)

Supports and helps; backs you up; is on your side; remembers your problem (19)

Uses team approach; helps group reach better decisions; facilitates cooperation (19)

Avoids close supervision; does not overboss; does not dictate or rule by the book (18)

Delegates authority; trusts group; relies on their judgment; permits group decisions; has faith in the creativity of others (17)

Communicates openly and honestly; tells you what he thinks; you can trust what he says (11)

Brings out best in his men; has common touch with the workers (8)

The interviews also provided data about the specific effects of the plant manager's new skills and methods:

Increased cooperation and coordination between all departments (21 comments)

Positive effect on foremen's behavior and growth as individuals (19)

Increased production and profits (11)

Better decisions and solutions (7)

Improvement in planning and tooling up (5)

More efficiency and cost reduction (4)

Improved communication (3)

These data, while admittedly subjective, were collected by an independent agency with no ax to grind. So the study tends to bolster my own confidence that the L.E.T. skills can be taught to leaders, that the new skills and methods readily become visible to the members of the leader's group as well as to his management associates, and that in time the skills and methods bring about positive outcomes in an organization, *even though no other leader in the company received the L.E.T. training.*

I am also hopeful that this book will help dispel some fruitless arguments and pervasive myths about leadership. Probably the most prevalent of these arguments is whether the "human-relations-oriented" (or person-centered) leader is better than the "task-oriented" (or production-centered) leader. The research clearly shows that the effective leader must be *both* a "human relations specialist" and a "task specialist." Leader effectiveness requires treating people decently, while at the same time successfully motivating them toward high performance in their work. One without the other doesn't work.

And there is an analogous argument about whether leaders should be strict or permissive. In Chapter VIII, I will point out the pitfalls of both approaches and caution leaders against either using their power to win conflicts or permitting group members to win at the expense of the leader losing. At the very core of my conception of effective leadership is a third alternative to "tough" or "soft" management. In the L.E.T. course it is called the No-lose Method for resolving conflicts of needs, so named because it produces solutions that result in "mutual need satisfaction"—no one loses. This is the ideal outcome that some writers, using "social exchange theory," describe as "an equitable exchange of benefits"—when solutions to conflicts *feel fair* to both leader and group members.

How to bring this about has not been clearly described in books on leadership. But in Chapters IX and X, you will learn, step by step, how to resolve conflicts with this No-lose Method.

Yet another issue has divided leaders into two camps—namely, the value of *meetings*. Some dislike meetings on the grounds they take too much time, rarely produce decisions, and are merely a "pooling of ignorance." For other leaders, meetings are a necessity; they are convinced they foster "participation," tap the creative potential of group members, and produce higher-quality decisions. I devote all of Chapter VII to meetings, for I am convinced that meetings are necessary but that they are often nonproductive, boring and time-consuming because leaders are unskilled and ineffective, or they use meetings for the wrong purposes.

I describe several types of meetings and suggest when each should be used and for what purpose. I offer 17 guidelines for making your problem-solving and decision-making meetings more efficient and productive. You'll find in these guidelines specific suggestions about such things as the frequency and duration of meetings, how to handle the minutes, how to develop an agenda and set priorities, what kinds of problems are inappropriate for groups, rules for decision-making, confidentiality, and methods for evaluating your meetings. I also provide you with some guidelines that will help your group members become more responsible participants at your meetings.

This book has three important features: (1) it attempts to synthesize the best thinking of social scientists and to draw from their research findings; (2) it presents a model (blueprint, if you will) of the ideal relationship between leaders and group members stated in nontechnical language that is understandable as well as usable; and (3) it offers specific skills and methods that leaders must learn to put the model to work.

This is not enough, however. My experience convinces me that no leader will improve his or her effectiveness very much without first coming to grips with the crucial issue of *power and authority*. Consequently, I have made a special effort to achieve clarity in my own thinking about power and authority. I have found widespread differences about the meaning of these terms among leaders in our L.E.T. classes and in the writings of professionals (which, of course, explains at least in part why people are sharply divided on whether leaders should or should not use their power or authority).

I believe I have succeeded in finding a way to clear up the confusion about power and authority. In Chapter VIII, I define three distinct kinds of authority, the first deriving from one's power (the means to punish or reward); the second from one's job definition; and the third from one's expertise and knowledge. The latter two seldom cause problems in human relationships, but the first almost inevitably is destructive to relationships, and in the long run also lowers motivation and productivity. Worse, when leaders use power they actually then lose the ability to influence their group members, a paradox I explain in the same chapter. How to influence people without using power is the key to leader effectiveness.

No person who has kept abreast of what is happening in organizations and institutions in our society can escape the conclusion that a revolution has started—a human relations revolution of great significance. In the words of Leonard Woodcock, at the time president of the United Auto Workers union, "Much has changed and is changing. Managers are recognizing that the human element is paramount." People want to be treated with respect and with dignity—as adults, not as children or ciphers; people are demanding to have a strong voice in their own working lives; people are less willing to be coerced and exploited; people want the right to achieve self-respect in their work and have work that is meaningful and rewarding; people are rebelling against inhuman working environments in very human ways—by job-hopping, absenteeism, apathetic attitudes, antagonism, and malicious mischief.

For leaders who already recognize "that the human element is paramount" and accept the predominant place of good human relationships in organizations, this book will provide invaluable skills and methods. If you want to avoid the destructive effects of coercing people with your power, you will find many nonpower alternatives in these pages. If you want to move away from making all decisions on your own, you'll find out how to develop a decision-making team. If you want open and honest two-way communication so that you can better influence your group members and they in turn better influence you, our Active Listening and I-message skills will accomplish that for you.

A final point: there is one thing this book will never do. It will not tell you what specific outcomes or results to expect from applying this leadership model. L.E.T. only teaches you *methodologies.* Through their use, different results will be achieved in different organizations, influenced by a variety of factors: what your organization does, the type of people you work with, the economic and financial limits within which your organization operates, and so on. Your new leadership skills may bring a reduction in costs and higher morale, as in one company I know. Or your human relations skills may bring similar results to those reported from the Volvo plant in Olofström, Sweden, by Pehr Gyllenhammar, president of Volvo, in his recent book *People at Work:*

Employee turnover was cut to one-quarter the previous average.

Absenteeism dropped to one-half the previous average.

Recruitment of new employees became easier.

Quality of product improved.

Labor productivity was maintained.

Or, as in my own small organization, your new leadership skills may result in such changes as these:

Adoption of "flexitime" scheduling that reduces absenteeism

A marked acceleration in the design and development of new training programs

Opening up of management meetings to any employee who wishes to participate

Reduction in status differentials between people at different levels in the organization

Assignment of every employee to a working group or "management team"

Or your change in leadership style may bring, as it has in some organizations, more mature and cooperative relations with unions; the institutionalization of a yearly "problem census"; installation of the Periodic Planning Conference in place of the traditional Merit Rating System; higher profits; installation of a profit-sharing system based on group performance; improved relations with customers or clients; the development of better communications systems or more efficient machinery; improvement of the physical environment for the workers; a job rotation system; placing responsibility for inspection with those who produce the product; work enlargement for menial jobs; longer vacations for older employees; putting production workers in charge of the speed of the assembly lines; hiring more women; hiring more handicapped; hiring more minorities; doing more supervisory training.

Any of these outcomes may be possible, for when leaders acquire the skills that enable them to release the productive potential of people and tap the collective capabilities of the group, who knows what positive results will be achieved? Some of them may move mountains.

II. BEING THE LEADER DOESN'T MAKE YOU ONE

FRANK Long was elected president of his service club. At about the same time, Robert Lathrop was appointed supervisor of all the tellers at his bank. Elizabeth Hall finally achieved her lifelong ambition of becoming vice-president in charge of sales in her company. After six years as a first-line supervisor in a manufacturing company, Bill Morrison was moved up to plant manager. Louise Lindley, by a large margin, was voted student body president at a midwestern college.

Their friends congratulated them and told them how much they deserved the new position. One phoned her husband and excitedly announced the good news. Another asked his wife to go out for dinner to celebrate. All felt proud of what they had achieved. Secretly, they all felt they had "arrived," "made it up the ladder," "got to the top."

These are the universal reactions of people who get appointed to positions of leadership. They feel, "I've made it." But in actuality, anyone who gets a leadership position has not made it. It is only the beginning.

Being the leader doesn't make you one. For after you

get to be the leader of a group, you're going to have to do a lot to earn the acceptance of the group members and have an influence on their behavior. Even more important, the acquisition of a leadership title—supervisor, department head, president, manager, or just plain boss—soon brings unexpected disappointments and uninvited problems. Undoubtedly you'll see evidence of jealousy on the part of some of your group members. Others may show resentment because they didn't get your job; in their eyes *you* didn't deserve the position, *they* did.

Also, you are likely to observe some subtle (and some not so subtle) changes in the way the group members relate to you. Some who only weeks ago were your friends now appear to avoid you and exclude you from their lunch groups. Others may start showing signs of being afraid of you; they act defensively, more guarded in their conversations, less frank in sharing their problems. You may even begin to detect some outright apple-polishing from certain members, or hypercritical behavior from others. And it won't be unusual to encounter negativism —unusually stubborn resistance to your new plans or helpful suggestions.

Becoming a group's leader almost inevitably brings about significant changes in your relationships with group members. People who previously reacted to you as a peer or friend suddenly have altered their posture toward you. You're "up there" and they're now "below" you; they "report to you"; you're "in charge."

Even if you were brought in from the outside to be made the leader of your group, be prepared to encounter a wide range of unfavorable responses—suspicion, distrust, hostility, subservience, passive resistance, insecurity. And don't overlook the possibility that someone might even like to see you fall flat on your face in your new job!

People come naturally to these built-in patterns of negative responses; they learned them when they were children. The leader "inherits" each group member's "inner child of the past." For each of us has a past history of being a child, intimately involved in multiple relationships with a variety of adults: parents, grandparents, schoolteachers, coaches, scout leaders, piano teachers, school principals, and of course the infamous assistant principal. All these adults had power and authority over us when we were youngsters, and most of them used it frequently. All children try out different behaviors to cope with these "authority figures." Some of their coping mechanisms prove effective, some ineffective. Those that work get used again and again, and so become habitual responses to all other adults who try to control and dominate them.

These coping mechanisms are seldom discarded when children pass into adolescence, or when they enter adulthood. They remain an integral part of the adult personality, to be called upon (or unconsciously triggered) whenever she or he enters a relationship with someone holding power or authority. So all adults in a very real sense harbor an "inner child of the past" that will strongly influence how they react to leaders.

When thrust into each new relationship with an authority figure, people naturally employ those same coping mechanisms that were built in by habitual use throughout their lifetime. This is why a new leader *inherits* the inner child of the past of each of his or her group members.* Their particular coping mechanisms are already present, ready to be used—the leader didn't cause them to be there. Nevertheless, because group members at first perceive most leaders as probable controllers and domina-

*While I am sensitive to the criticism of sexist writing, I have found myself unable totally to avoid traditional sexist forms in our language. This book is written for both men and women, who in my opinion are equally able to become effective leaders. Where possible, I have used the plural "leaders," permitting the pronoun "their." Sometimes I have chosen to use "him or her" or "her and him."

tors, that's the way they will respond to him or her, *even though the leader may have no intention of using power and authority.*

Undoubtedly you will recognize most of the coping mechanisms in the following list, and you'll be tempted to identify the particular ones you most often employed as a youngster, as well as those you find yourself still using as an adult:

1. Resistance, defiance, rebellion, negativism

2. Resentment, anger, hostility

3. Aggression, retaliation, striking back, ridiculing the authority figure

4. Lying, hiding feelings

5. Blaming others, tattling, cheating

6. Dominating, bossing, or bullying those with less power

7. Needing to win, hating to lose, perfectionism

8. Forming alliances, organizing against the authority figure

9. Submission, obedience, compliance, subservience

10. Apple-polishing, courting favor, buttering up the authority figure

11. Conformity, fear of trying something new or creative, requiring prior assurance of success, dependence on authority figure

12. Withdrawing, escaping, fantasizing, regressing

13. Getting sick

14. Crying

Is it now more clear why, when you become a leader, you haven't made it? In fact, it might be said that you've had it! Even before you get much of a chance to earn the leadership of your group, in the eyes of the members you have a new identity—a potential controller and dominator. And even before you make any actual use of your authority or power, group members are already pro-grammed and ready to cope with it, using some combina-tion of the above coping mechanisms.

Certainly I don't intend to discourage anyone from as-piring to become a leader. Rather, I want to be quite realistic about the unique dynamics that govern the rela-tionship between leaders and group members. And prin-cipally I want to underscore the thesis of this book: *being the leader does not make you one, because leaders don't automatically get the respect and acceptance of their group members; so in order to earn the leadership of their group and have a positive influence on the group mem-bers, leaders must learn some specific skills and methods.*

WHAT MAKES A LEADER?

"Leaders are born, not made." That's what most people thought, until social scientists began to make lead-ership a legitimate subject for intensive investigation, no more than 40 or 50 years ago. Back in the old days, when strong social class barriers made it next to impossible for just anyone to become a leader, it appeared to most peo-ple that leadership was *inherited,* since leaders emerged so frequently within the same favored families. As class barriers crumbled and it became obvious that leaders were coming from all strata of society, common sense told us that leadership was much more complex than being born with the right genes or in the proper families.

If not the right combination of genes, then perhaps all leaders possess certain traits or characteristics acquired through their upbringing or education. This notion started a search for the *universal traits of leaders.* But then hundreds of studies showed no trait differences between leaders and nonleaders, which all but killed the theory that leadership was a product of certain attributes residing within all leaders.

A major breakthrough came when social scientists began to look at leadership as an *interaction* between leaders and their followers. After all, they reasoned, it is the follower who in the last analysis either accepts or rejects the influence of the leader. The key question became: why do followers accept and why do they reject? What goes on in this interaction?

Obviously, you can't be a leader without followers. You won't for long be a group leader without having group members who accept your influence, guidance, and direction. But how does a leader acquire followers? The answer to this basic question emerges clearly when we understand the *needs* all human beings possess and how they struggle to *satisfy those needs*. Somewhat oversimplified, here is an explanation of how leaders acquire followers.

1. To survive, every person is engaged in a continuous struggle to satisfy needs or relieve tension.

2. Some *means* is required to satisfy a need (tools, food, money, physical strength, knowledge, etc.).

3. Most needs of individuals are satisfied in *relationships with people or groups,* so people and groups become the *means* we rely on most heavily for the satisfaction of our needs. (We do not grow our own food, make our own clothes, get our education by ourselves, etc.).

4. People actively seek out those relationships in which the other person is seen as having the *means* for satisfying their needs.

5. People join groups, then, because they hope that membership will offer them the means for satisfying their needs. Conversely, they leave groups when they no longer get their needs satisfied.

6. Group members accept influence and direction of a leader only if they regard him or her as a person through whose means they will get their needs satisfied. People follow (and permit their activities to be directed by) a leader whom they believe will get them what they need or want.

It follows that a leader earns and retains his or her role as a leader only if in the eyes of the group members "following the leader" holds out the promise that they will get their needs met. This book will identify and describe the critical attitudes, skills, methods, and procedures required to make this promise a reality. No longer is it such a mystery how certain persons become effective in earning and retaining leadership of their groups and how others do not. Through research and observation, social scientists have identified many of the critical requirements of effective leadership. It is my aim to organize this knowledge so that it is more easily *understandable* to those who aspire to become leaders and more *available* for their use.

THE LEADER'S DILEMMA

Acquiring followers through meeting the needs of group members* does not tell the whole story of effective leadership. The other side of the coin is that leaders must be successful in getting their own needs satisfied.

People seldom seek leadership positions solely to satisfy the needs of group members. Leaders are human, too. And they have the usual human needs for status, achievement, higher pay, recognition, self-esteem, security, and acceptance—in fact, usually the same needs as their group members. If they don't find ways of satisfying these needs in their leadership position, they will not want to remain there very long. Even when leaders continue to tolerate a job long after they find that many of their needs are *not* satisfied, they soon find themselves incapable of putting forth all the effort required to do what they must do to

*Throughout this book I shall use the terms "group members," "workers," and "subordinates" interchangeably. While I dislike the latter term, it enjoys such common usage that dropping it seems unrealistic. I shall also use a variety of terms for leaders—such as "superiors," "bosses," "supervisors," "managers," and "administrators."

ensure that their group members' needs are satisfied.

The explanation is obvious: people will continue to expend energy doing things that benefit others only if they feel they are receiving "reciprocal benefits." There is always a limit to one-way sharing of benefits in human relationships. You can think of this principle in terms of "I'll scratch your back if you scratch mine."

The "full cup principle" is also at work here: to be able to continue giving to others (letting them drink from my cup), I must have a full cup and find ways of replenishing myself (keeping my cup relatively full). The importance of this principle is well understood by professional "helping agents" (therapists and counselors), who find their own helping capabilities seriously reduced when they experience troubles and need-deprivations in their own personal lives. This is why so many professional therapists find it necessary to retain their own therapists to keep their professional cup relatively full.

Then, too, one of the strongest needs of all leaders operating in an organizational setting is to look good in the eyes of their own bosses. True, a leader's self-esteem is derived largely from inputs and evaluations of his or her superiors. And more important, unless leaders meet the expectations and objectives of their bosses (are perceived as effective in helping the organization reach its goals), they will be under the threat of being demoted or discharged.

Consequently, leaders working within a formal organization are caught in a dilemma—they must meet the needs of the organization, *as well as* satisfy the needs of their group members. The trick lies in learning how to balance the needs from both directions, so as to be perceived as effective by both superiors and group members. As anyone knows who has worked in a formal organization, this is not an easy task, because organizational needs are primarily for increased productivity and efficiency, while the group members' needs are often those that motivate them to resist pressure for increased productivity and efficiency.

Numerous studies of leadership in hierarchical organizations strongly indicate that effective leaders need one set of skills to meet their own needs (and those of their superiors for productivity and efficiency) and another set of quite different skills to satisfy the needs of group members. For the present, I'll describe these two sets of skills in very general terms:

A. Skills to meet group members' needs

1. Behavior that increases group members' self-esteem and personal worth.

2. Behavior that increases group cohesiveness and team spirit.

B. Skills to meet organizational needs

1. Behavior that motivates productivity and the achievement of group goals.

2. Behavior that helps members reach goals: planning, scheduling, coordinating, problem-solving, providing resources.

An effective leader cannot be only a "human relations specialist" (meeting members' needs) nor only a "productivity specialist" (meeting organizational needs). *He or she must be both.* Even more important, the effective leader must also acquire the flexibility or sensitivity to know when and where to employ these quite diverse skills to achieve *mutual satisfaction of the needs of group members and the needs of the leader.* Finally, the effective leader must learn skills to resolve the inevitable conflicts that arise between these two competing sources of needs.

This book aims to show leaders how they can become more effective in producing this essential state of *mutual need satisfaction;* how they can become more flexible and sensitive through fostering more honest communication with their superiors as well as with their own group members; and how they can employ an equitable (or "no-lose") method of resolving conflicts of needs that will greatly reduce resentment, hostility, and alienation in their relationships with others.

WHAT PEOPLE NEED FROM THEIR GROUP

Leaders of groups earn their positions of leadership by doing things that, in the eyes of the members, make their hopes come true that their needs will be satisfied. Let me stress again: *you can't be a leader without having group members.* And group members will accept your direction and influence only if you help them get their needs satisfied.

It sounds simple enough, but first leaders must learn exactly what their group members need. Only then can they decide what to do to satisfy those needs in exchange for the members' performing certain services or functions for the organization. This equitable exchange is the key to leadership.

What do people need from their group? Early "scientific management" specialists thought that individuals worked primarily for personal financial gain. This is the "economic man" theory. Later research conclusively demonstrated that people need much more from their groups—among other things, the acceptance of other members, a feeling of achievement and accomplishment, social interaction with other members, and the opportunity to achieve social status from participating in the group.

It is therefore much more accurate to think of "socioeconomic man," a concept that acknowledges that leaders have a wide range of incentives to offer group members to attract them to the group. To retain them in the group as productive group members, effective leaders must satisfy more than simply the financial needs of their people.

A useful way of describing the needs of people is in the form of a hierarchy with several different levels. The pioneering psychologist Abraham Maslow, then professor of psychology at Brandeis University, constructed a five-tiered pyramid that represents the relative importance of five different kinds of human needs to an individual:

The Level I needs, such as thirst, hunger, and warmth, are the most important (or "prepotent"), for they must be predominantly satisfied before a person will be motivated to try to satisfy the needs at the next level. The Level II needs (security and safety) must be predominantly satisfied before a person will be motivated to seek satisfaction for the higher-level needs, and so on up the pyramid. For example, a primitive man who is hungry will be highly motivated to stalk a wild animal to obtain food, even risking his life (ignoring safety and security needs). After killing the animal and eating what he needs and now motivated to satisfy his security needs, he may cure the remaining meat and store it for future consumption (safety and security needs). When plenty is stored away, he then might think of asking friends to come over and share his food (needs for acceptance and social interaction). When those needs are met, he may decide to experiment with a new and more flavorful way of preparing his food (needs for achievement, self-esteem). Finally, if those needs are reasonably satisfied he might decide to paint pictures of the animals he has killed on the walls of his cave (need for self-actualization).

The implications of Maslow's theory of hierarchical needs are of great importance to leaders.

1. Groups and organizations do not always provide opportunities for their members to satisfy Level IV and Level V needs, especially for people at lower levels whose jobs are quite rigidly defined or routine, whose activities are almost totally controlled, and whose freedom for personal direction, making decisions, and taking initiative are very limited.

2. When leaders exercise arbitrary power, group members may feel afraid of censure or continually feel insecure in their jobs. With their security and safety needs not satisfied, they are thus stuck at Level II, unmotivated to achieve and meet their social needs and their need for competence and self-esteem.

3. Different groups members may be operating at different need levels at the same time or in the same situation. In a staff meeting one subordinate may be tired (Level I); another may want the group to get something accomplished (Level IV); still others may be talking and joking with each other (Level III).

4. Level I and Level II needs are seldom very potent

motivators in our affluent society, for subordinates already are getting most of their physiological needs satisfied (minimum wage laws) and are often free of the insecurity of being fired (protection of unions). This is why it seldom works when leaders try to motivate or control group members by using warnings or threats of being fired.

5. If workers have little opportunity to satisfy their needs at Levels III, IV, and V *on the job,* they will seek opportunities *off the job* to satisfy their needs for social interaction, achievement, and self-actualization (through sports, hobbies, and social clubs). This is why many people put forth only just enough energy to keep their jobs and receive their pay; in addition, they feel alienated from (or uninvolved in) the organization.

6. To be motivated toward high achievement and accomplishment (Level IV), members need leaders who already have seen to it that *(a)* they receive a wage that seems equitable, *(b)* they have a feeling of job security, and *(c)* the group provides them opportunity for social interaction, friendship, and a feeling of being understood and accepted (Levels I, II, and III needs are being satisfied).

7. One of the principal benefits to members from having a leader who makes it possible for them to participate in group problem-solving and decision-making is that such activity gives them a great deal of opportunity to satisfy their social and interactional needs (Level III), their needs for self-esteem and status in the organization (Level IV), and on occasion their needs for self-actualization and self-development (Level V).

A refinement of Maslow's concept provides leaders with even more insight into the needs of group members. It is the two-factor theory of motivation developed from the research of Frederick Herzberg, formerly at Carnegie Institute of Technology, more recently at the University of Utah. He collected evidence of two relatively independent factors: (1) certain factors operating in a work group situation act as *obstacles* to need satisfaction and become irritants, or *"dissatisfiers"*; (2) other factors are viewed as providers of need satisfaction and become gratifiers of needs, or *"satisfiers."*

Acting as *obstacles* to need satisfaction ("dissatisfiers") were:

1. Poor interpersonal relationships with superiors.
2. Poor interpersonal relationships with peers.
3. Inadequate technical supervision.
4. Poor company policies and administration.
5. Poor working conditions.
6. Problems in workers' personal lives.

Acting as *providers* of need satisfaction ("satisfiers") were:

1. Achievement
2. Recognition
3. The work itself
4. Responsibility
5. Advancement

The *absence of the dissatisfiers* seldom produced satisfaction—for example, *good* working conditions seldom produced feelings of satisfaction. However, *poor* working conditions did produce feelings of dissatisfaction. But only the *presence of the satisfiers* (achievement, recognition, etc.) brought feelings of satisfaction.

These studies strongly suggest—and this is extremely important to leaders—that for group members to feel motivated toward high productivity and be satisfied in their jobs, *the work itself must be rewarding.* The job must provide opportunity for growth, responsibility, recognition, and advancement. These requirements sound very much like Maslow's Level III, IV, and V needs, and so provide further support for my earlier assertion that the effective leader needs to learn well the skills and methods that enable group members to meet their highest-level needs—*self-esteem* from achievement on the job and from the recognition of that achievement, as well as *self-actualization* (the feeling of utilizing one's potential). These skills and methods will be described in detail in subsequent chapters.

These significant findings may not apply quite the same way with workers at lower levels of an organization. They are much more likely to feel a strong sense of *deprivation* if their Level I and II needs are not satisfied (poor pay, job insecurity). Consequently, leaders of such groups can never ignore indications that group members may be feeling their wages are inequitable or that they are insecure about keeping their jobs.

Comparable findings to those of Herzberg were obtained in a six-year study of motivation conducted by M. Scott Myers, an industrial psychologist at Texas Instruments. The results were summarized in the *Harvard Business Review* as follows:

What motivates employees to work effectively? A challenging job which allows a feeling of achievement, responsibility, growth, advancement, enjoyment of work itself, and earned recognition.

What dissatisfies workers? Mostly factors which are peripheral to the job—work rules, lighting, coffee breaks, titles, seniority rights, wages, fringe benefits, and the like.

When do workers become dissatisfied? When opportunities for meaningful achievement are eliminated and they become sensitized to their environment and begin to find fault.

Myers, like Herzberg, identified the same two kinds of employee needs that supervisors must satisfy, but named them Motivation Needs, which are task-centered, and Maintenance Needs, which are relatively peripheral to the work itself.

Myers' study offers further validation of the point I have been emphasizing all along, namely: the effective supervisor must have the skills of a *task specialist* (skills of planning and organizing work) as well as the skills of a *human relations specialist* (skills of identifying and solving sources of member dissatisfaction). The effective leader is task-centered *and* people-centered. Group members want to be on a winning team, but never at the expense of injuries to their self-worth or self-respect.

THE LEADER AS A PROBLEM-SOLVER

It has also been helpful to me to think of the principal function of a group leader as *facilitating problem-solving*. Groups need a leader to see to it that their problems get solved. One could make the case that a completely problem-free work group would not even need a leader—at least not very often. If a group could always function efficiently and productively so that its members always experienced a sense of achievement, group cohesion, high self-esteem, and personal worth, obviously there would be little need for a "supervisor." Only when groups have problems do they sorely need leaders —that is, either when the members are having problems getting their personal needs met or when the group is causing the leader problems because it is failing to attain the goals of the organization.

I have designed a pictorial or graphic scheme for showing the relationship between these two kinds of problems and it will help you tie together all the ideas drawn from

Maslow and Herzberg. Put yourself for a moment in the shoes of a group leader and imagine that whenever you observe one of your group members, his or her behavior will always show through a rectangular window that you hold in front of your face. Now imagine that the window has two panes or sections: one for behaviors of the group member that are acceptable to you because they cause you no problem (the top section of your window), the other for behaviors that are unacceptable to you because they are causing you a problem (the bottom part of your rectangle).

Carrie, one of your group members, is working diligently at her desk completing an assignment. Because that behavior is in no way causing you a problem, you locate it in the top part of your rectangle for Carrie:

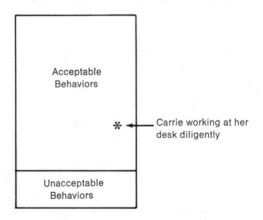

Recently, Jerry, another group member, has been showing a strong need to come to your office to check with you or get your approval on matters you feel he is perfectly capable of solving independently. You feel he is wasting your time (and his) and being overly dependent. This particular behavior is unacceptable to you, so you locate it in the bottom part of your rectangle for Jerry:

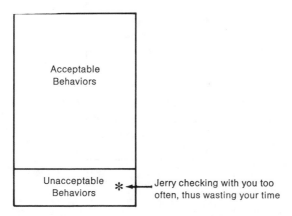

This is a useful way for thinking about the behavior of any group member, as we shall see. First, it forces you to become aware of your honest *feelings* about a specific behavior: do you accept it or do you not? It also signals when the other person's behavior is causing you a problem. However, it doesn't yet tell you what to do about the problem. That comes later, in the next chapter.

You should also know that in your "behavior rectangle" the line dividing its two areas does not remain stationary. It moves up and down frequently: (1) because of things going on in you (how you are feeling today), (2) because of where you are (the particular environment in which the behavior occurs), and (3) because of the different characteristics of different group members (some people are easier to accept than others).

To illustrate, on days when you are well and rested and feeling good about yourself, your rectangles for subordinates usually show a large area of acceptable behaviors, like this:

"Good" day

Comes the day when you are tired, feeling like you're getting a cold, or upset about progress on a report you're writing, your rectangle could very well look like this:

"Bad" day

Just *where* the other person's behavior occurs also affects your rectangle markedly. At the company's Christmas party, for example, your rectangle for each of your subordinates will probably have a much larger area of acceptable behaviors than usual:

Office Party

In this environment, the raucous behavior of subordinates after several cocktails would be quite acceptable; obviously, many of the same behaviors would never be acceptable during working hours.

Naturally, your behavior rectangle is further influenced by the particular characteristics of the other person. You may feel much more accepting of behaviors of an old-time employee whose idiosyncrasies you've gotten used to than the behaviors of a brand-new employee:

Old-time employee   New employee

Your rectangle tells you that you can't be "consistent" in your feelings about group member behavior. You're human, and your human feelings (of acceptance or unacceptance) will change considerably from day to day, from situation to situation, and from person to person. Many people, once placed in a leadership position, assume a role and feel they must repress or hide their human-ness to be consistent.

The behavioral rectangle is still not complete until we deal with another kind of behavior of group members. As a leader you will observe behaviors of group members that will signal that *they* are experiencing a problem meeting their own needs. Such behavior may not cause *you* a problem, at least in any tangible or concrete way, but it is clear that your subordinates are experiencing some kind of personal problem—some need is not being satisfied or there is a threat to them of need deprivation. You will generally get verbal clues, such as

"I'm upset" or "I'm mad"

"I'm unhappy" or "I'm dissatisfied"

"What a day this has been!" or "I should've stayed in bed!"

"Screw the company!" or "What the hell do they expect of us?"

Or their clues may be more behavioral and less direct, such as:

Acting sulky or depressed

Acting nervous, touchy, or hypersensitive

Avoiding talking to you

Not looking you in the eye

Acting tense, fearful, anxious

Griping frequently

Daydreaming or becoming forgetful

Such behaviors belong in a special area of your rectangle, labeled *"Behaviors indicating subordinate has a problem"*:

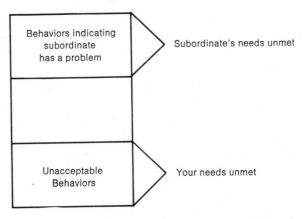

To be consistent we should relabel the bottom third of the rectangle, *"Behaviors causing you a problem"*:

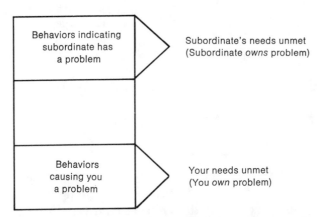

This leaves the middle area of the rectangle—I call it the *No-problem Area*—for behaviors of a subordinate that do not indicate he or she has, or "owns," a problem, and do not cause you a problem. So in the No-problem Area you will place all behaviors that suggest your subordinate is experiencing satisfaction of needs, and so are *you:* the area of "mutual need satisfaction." These are the times when *productive work* is being done* because there are no problems in the leader-subordinate relationship.

We can now restate the principal function of an effective leader in somewhat different terms: *to maximize productive work time and achieve mutual need satisfaction.*

The essential task of the leader, then, is to initiate problem-solving, both when subordinates own problems and when the leader owns problems, and the goal is to increase the size of the No-problem Area or increase the amount of time for productive work. But remember: dealing effectively with these two kinds of problems requires two different kinds of skills:

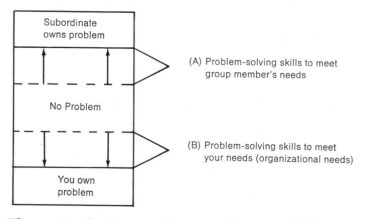

The rectangle diagram also provides a visual depiction of my earlier verbal description of what research studies proved: effective leaders need to meet the needs of group members as well as the organization. The rectangle also represents and underscores my subsequent definition of

*I use the term "productive work" in a generic way to stand for whatever activities are required to attain the goals of the group. In a group organized for recreation, productive work time might even be time to "play."

a leader as one whose principal function is problem-solving.

The areas left in the top and bottom areas of the rectangle are intended to represent what must be obvious to the reader—leaders will never be able to meet *all* the unmet needs (problems) of subordinates nor reach a point where *all* their own problems (and the organization's problems) are solved. That's an ideal worth striving for, but it is unlikely to be reached by leaders, at least in any organization I know.

III. DOING IT YOURSELF—OR WITH THE GROUP'S HELP

On becoming the leader of a group, few people seem able to resist the temptation to grab the reins, make a flying start, and plunge into the task of trying to solve all the problems alone. Understandably, the initial concern of most new leaders is to justify, as quickly as possible, their selection to the superiors who appointed them. They want to look good, and the sooner the better. After all, what is a leader for if not to step right in and "take charge"? In the military the expression is "take command."

Unfortunately, rushing in to take charge can get leaders into hot water. Eager to produce quick reforms, instant cures, and dramatic increases in productivity, leaders succumb to the well-known "new broom" temptation, with high expectations of sweeping clean the mess left by the group's previous boss. Yet seldom can leaders do it on their own without the group members' willingness and cooperation, neither of which is likely to be immediately forthcoming. Groups resist change and hang on tenaciously to their habitual ways. These "group norms" exert a strong influence on the behavior of the group members.

For example, groups generally develop their own standards of what is a "fair day's work" or a "productivity norm," which are clearly understood by the members and informally enforced within the group. Any action of the leader that is perceived as a threat to the maintenance of this norm is strongly resisted, *especially if the action of the leader is regarded as arbitrary.*

Another way of looking at these resistive forces within groups is in terms of "fair exchange." Groups strongly resist actions of a leader that might upset the group definition of an equitable cost/benefit ratio—i.e., getting fair benefits (wages, for example) in relation to the amount of energy (cost) exerted on the job. A new boss with a new broom may be looked upon as upsetting this ratio, and the group will want to protect itself against being exploited by the organization.

Groups also strongly resist the introduction of new methods and procedures, especially if they are arbitrarily and unilaterally instituted by the leader. We all know how people get used to doing things in a certain way, so when they have to learn a new way it often seems that this requires more energy output than the group members are willing to give.

Many eager new leaders take the posture of a vigilant "overseer"—they're going to keep very close tabs on their group members, nothing is going to escape them, and mistakes just won't be made because they will be "on top of things." Such "oversupervising" takes many forms, such as:

Requiring detailed activity or progress reports

Requiring group members to get the leader's approval before sending out letters, implementing plans, or making decisions

Taking over tasks previously assigned to group members to make sure they are done "right"

Making members "go through the leader" before initiating contacts outside the group.

One of the inevitable effects of oversupervision is resentment against the leader's arbitrary use of power. Another effect is passive resistance to the new demands (the activity reports somehow never seem to get turned in). Even worse for the group, oversupervision makes members too dependent on the leader. They start coming to the leader with *every* problem. Their self-motivation drops; their initiative is stifled. They won't grow in their jobs; the leader finds himself overloaded and overburdened, having to do everything himself. The work *group* now becomes a "one-man (or one-woman) operation." New leaders who try to oversupervise in their new job find out too late that they really *are* going it alone, without the benefit of all the resources of the group.

"THE WISDOM OF THE GROUP"

Thinking again of effective leaders as persons with skills in problem-solving, I must emphasize that leaders need not assume full responsibility to problem-solve *alone;* rather, they can enlist the resources of the group members to help them. In theory at least, the ideal group would marshal the creative resources of *every* member (including the leader, of course) as it faces its problems and searches for the best solutions. Not every member *needs to be involved* in all problem-solving, but in the ideal group the resources of all members are *available* when appropriate or necessary.

My experience as a consultant to organizations convinces me that most leaders greatly underestimate the wealth of knowledge, ideas, and ingenuity lying untapped in the heads of group members. Also, my personal experience as head of my own organization has provided me with almost daily evidence of the "wisdom of the group." By this I do not mean that for every problem I must enlist the resources of the *entire* group. I rely on different group members at different times to help me carry out the problem-solving function—sometimes it's one member, sometimes several, sometimes my staff of immediate subordinates, and only rarely the entire organization.

For solving critical or complex problems I almost always harness the brains and experiences of one or more members of my organization. And when problems look as if they affect all divisions, they are routinely brought up in regularly scheduled staff meetings attended by the heads of all divisions, plus anyone else who wants to attend. (More about regularly scheduled staff meetings in Chapter VII.)

I'm hardly alone in my views about the wisdom of collective thinking. K. K. Paluev, then research and development engineer for the General Electric Company, wrote this about the "collective genius" of groups contributing to several projects involving the design of huge power transformers:

These achievements could not have been achieved were it not for the ability of the organization to integrate its diversified faculties for every type of problem that confronts it. . . .

. . . Since it is impossible to obtain enough individuals who are "complete genii," industrial management and all coworkers must be content with the fact that they themselves as well as their colleagues fall short of perfection.

Alfred Marrow, when chairman of the board of the Harwood Manufacturing Corporation, came to this conclusion about the need for collaboration in organizations:

At one time, the educational gap between rank-and-file workers and company executives was wide and deep. This is no longer true and the gap will become less marked in the years ahead. . . . It is now common that employees are more technically skilled than their supervisors. . . .

Today the greatest challenge confronting a conscientious executive has become the collaboration of people, particularly his managerial staff. He must turn his staff into an effective team of men who pull for the company, collaboratively but in their individual ways, instead of being "every man for himself."

Today it is seldom questioned *whether* a leader should use the creative resources of group members to solve problems; so many effective leaders do just that, either informally or formally (as in staff meetings). The critical questions are: when to get group member participation, whom to select, what kinds of problems require it, how and by whom the final decisions are made, and how to handle conflicts. I will address these questions in detail later, and offer skills and methods for handling such issues.

WHY BUILD A TEAM?

Some leaders may enlist the help of individual group members for problem-solving from time to time on an as-needed and informal basis, yet do not consciously attempt to develop their entire work group into a problem-solving and decision-making "management team." To accomplish this goal, leaders need to take additional steps, and also learn how to conduct effective staff meetings. (See Chapter VII for the specific skills required for conducting decision-making meetings.)

The necessity of building a management team is central in my concept of leader effectiveness. And there are many cogent arguments to support this position:

1. Individual members of an organization will be more identified with the goals of the organization and concerned about its success if they participate in making decisions about those goals and how to reach them.

2. Being a member of a management team gives group members a feeling of greater control over their lives; it frees them from the fear of the leader's arbitrary use of power.

3. When group members participate in solving the group's problems, they learn a great deal about the technical complexities of whatever the group's task is; they learn from each other, as well as from the leader. *Developing a management team is the best kind of ongoing staff development* (in-service training).

4. Participation on a management team provides opportunities for the members to *satisfy many of their higher-level needs* for self-esteem, acceptance, and self-actualization.

5. A management team helps break down *status differentials* between the members and the leader, which fosters more open and honest communication between members and leader.

6. A management team becomes the principal vehicle enabling the leader to exemplify the kind of leadership behavior he or she wants the group members to learn and use in relationships with *their* subordinates. In this way effective leadership moves down through the levels of organizations.

7. Higher-quality decisions often result from bringing into play the combined resources of the work group.

A rather widespread misunderstanding exists about the "management team" concept. I use the term to mean the *entire work group as an integral unit (rather than an aggregate of individuals), governing itself within the area of freedom allowed by its position in the organizational hierarchy.* The president of an organization and all the executives reporting directly to him or her would be a management team. But a supervisor and all the workers reporting to her would also be a management team. Large organizations are made up of several or many interlocking management teams, as shown in the figure below:

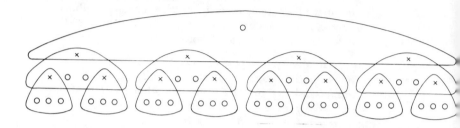

In this figure, every member of the organization belongs to a management team, and some members (called "linking pins") belong to two. In one, the person is a leader; in the other, a group member. Linking pins are identified by *X*.

As will be documented in subsequent chapters, the success of a management team will depend greatly on the leader's skills in (1) fostering open and honest communication within the team, (2) resolving conflicts so nobody loses (the "No-lose Method"), (3) conducting efficient and productive decision-making meetings, (4) being an effective "task specialist" as well as a "human relations specialist," and (5) being a strong and effective advocate for his or her group members in the team that operates one level above the one in which the leader is a group member.

Most important for team building and effective team functioning is the leaders' success in reducing any status barriers between themselves and their subordinates. No other concept is more important than this. It is at the very core of my definition of leadership effectiveness. I'll say it in the briefest way: *effective leaders must behave in such a way that they come to be perceived almost as another group member; at the same time they must help all group members feel as free as the leader to make contributions and perform needed functions in the group.*

If leaders are to be successful in building an effective team, they must learn specific skills that foster a climate allowing subordinates to feel free to speak up, make suggestions, participate actively in problem-solving—yes, and criticize the ideas of the leader. Leaders must avoid prestige-seeking behaviors that tend to increase the status differences between themselves and their group members: acting in a superior manner, behaving arrogantly, using power arbitrarily. Research has shown that such behaviors will decrease interaction between leaders and members because of the tendency of the less powerful to increase the distance between themselves and the more powerful. Group members draw away from leaders who make them feel inadequate or lower their self-esteem.

It is indeed a paradox that *effective leaders act very much like group members and effective group members act like group leaders.* The surest sign of a group's effectiveness comes when the person who at first was treated as the leader later becomes seen almost as another group member. In an effective group, the contributions of all members will be evaluated on merit, not on the prestige of the contributor. Only when the leader becomes like another member will his or her own contributions be accepted *or* rejected, just like those of any other member, solely on merit. Group members then feel free to say to the leader "That's a good idea" rather than think "That *should* be a good idea because it is the leader's."

When leaders achieve this "another member" status, they actually *increase* the contributions they can make to the group, because their ideas will get evaluated like those of other members. At first this may seem completely contrary to fact because we ordinarily think that people can have a more positive effect on a group if they hold on to the prestige and power of the *leader position.* A real case can be made for rejecting this traditional belief. We do know that leaders often have more effect on a group than any of its members, but what kind of effect?

For one thing, their contributions are often accepted uncritically by members because they feel the leader *must* know more than they. So if his or her contributions are *not* all good (and this is a sure bet with most leaders), the total effectiveness of the group is reduced. We also know that sometimes a leader's contributions are *rejected* solely because they come from the leader. This is a common reaction to authority—as when children are "negative" to their parents. If some of the leader's ideas *are* good ones, yet are rejected by the group, again the net effect will be to reduce the total effectiveness of the group. This is why leaders actually gain more freedom to make a useful contribution after they have reduced or removed the status or prestige differential that existed between them and the group members. If they are successful, they become another productive group member, trying to make contributions whenever their knowledge or experience is appropriate and useful to the group.

WHO IS RESPONSIBLE?

Many leaders resist the idea of developing a management team because they feel ultimately "responsible" for the success or failure of their work group and therefore believe that they must make all the decisions and call the shots.

Obviously, in formal organizations leaders are in fact held responsible for how their work groups perform, although I prefer to use the term "accountable" rather than "responsible." Certainly, if a work group is not performing adequately to meet the needs of the organization, the

leader cannot expect to be excused by superiors by putting all the blame on the group members. The leader *is*
held accountable, not the group.

Harry Truman's desk plaque, "The buck stops here," is
appropriate for the desks of all leaders. They must accept
accountability for the groups they lead. (They really can't
be "responsible" for group members, for each member in
reality must be responsible for herself or himself.)

Yet leaders can decide they prefer accountability based
on decisions in which subordinates participate, just as do-
it-yourself leaders accept accountability based on decisions they make alone. *How* decisions get made, then, is
not at all relevant to a leader's accountability (superiors
obviously hold leaders accountable for *all* decisions).
Those leaders who consciously decide to make decisions
with the participation of group members do so because
they feel that this results in high-quality decisions for
which they are quite willing to be accountable.

However, there is a great deal of controversy among
leaders about the quality of group decisions. Does participative decision-making and problem-solving really
yield high-quality decisions? Some leaders are convinced
that groups are unable to make good decisions; they cite
the overworked joke, "A camel is a horse created by a
committee." To some leaders it is inconceivable that a
group is capable of making wise decisions. To them, wise
decisions are made only by wise *leaders.*

The problem is invariably formulated incorrectly in the
first place. The argument is usually over whether the best
decisions are made by group members *or* by the group
leader. Stated this way, the group members are pitted
against the group leader, which often does stack the cards
against the members because leaders often do have more
information or experience than members.

Let me rephrase the question: can a leader (*without* the
resources of the group members) make wiser decisions

than the group *(including the leader)*? Now we pit the total group with all its available resources against the leader with only his or her limited resources. If we place this problem in the family situation, the commonly accepted belief that "Father knows best" could be challenged by a perceptive youngster who might retort, "Yes, but does father know better than father plus children?"

Even when a group solves problems and makes decisions utilizing the resources of all its members, there is no assurance that all solutions and decisions will be of highest quality. But the same is true when leaders solve problems or make decisions alone. Group solutions and decisions, like individual solutions and decisions, can range from bad to excellent. In Chapter VII I will offer specific methods for increasing the effectiveness of group problem-solving so that high-quality decisions are more likely.

DON'T SOLVE PROBLEMS; SEE THAT PROBLEMS GET SOLVED

In Chapter II I emphasized that effective leaders are skilled in problem-solving, but I didn't mean that leaders themselves must come up with most solutions, even though some assume this burdensome responsibility, priding themselves that no problem ever escapes their attention. This posture exacts a high price. Such leaders end up running a "one-man show" and overseeing dependent group members who have not been allowed to develop their problem-solving capabilities.

Common sense tells us no leader can have all the answers. In most work groups, problems are too numerous and complex to be solved by the resources of the leader alone. This is as true for technical (job-related) problems as it is for human problems, which are often more complex—particularly when it concerns a personal problem of a group member or an interpersonal conflict between two members.

An effective group leader, then, does not need to *solve* problems, but to *see to it that they get solved.* Instead of being a good problem-solver, the effective leader must be a good *facilitator of problem-solving.* Central to this conception of leader effectiveness is the requirement that the leader understands that problem-solving is a *process* and that he or she must learn certain skills that will get that process started and take it to a successful completion.

The problem-solving process involves six separate steps:

I.   Identifying and defining the problem

II. Generating alternative solutions

III. Evaluating the alternative solutions

IV. Decision-making

V.   Implementing the decision

VI. Following up to evaluate the solution

In Chapter VII I will show how a leader may enlist participation of group members in any or all of these steps. Clearly, leaders need help in identifying and defining problems in the work group (Step I), for they are often unaware of problems. As for generating alternative solutions (Step II), subordinates, when given the chance, can come up with scores of creative alternative solutions in brainstorming meetings commonly used in organizations. Step III utilizes subordinates' varied experience as well as their cognitive skills to assess the relative worth of alternative solutions. When a final commitment to the "best solution" is made in Step IV, this often requires all available brainpower of the group. Subordinate participation in Step V is often crucial because many decisions must be implemented by the group members and they want a voice in determining *who* does *what* and by *when.* In

Step VI, the follow-up evaluation to assess whether the solution actually solved the problem, subordinates must often collect the data required to make such an evaluation.

For certain kinds of problems, especially personal problems "owned by a subordinate," the leader may not participate directly in the problem-solving process, but acts *primarily* as facilitator of the subordinate's own internal problem-solving process—helping the subordinate "talk through" the six steps independently, very much the way professional counselors do when they help people with personal problems. In the next chapter I'll explain this counseling function of the leader and describe the skill of Active Listening, which is so potent in getting subordinates to solve problems on their own.

When leaders learn the skills of a problem-solving *facilitator* (seeing that problems get solved), it actually makes their job much easier than if they attempt to solve all the problems on their own—a role that would require leaders to have all the answers, be omniscient, be equipped with inhuman intelligence or have an inexhaustible storehouse of knowledge and experience. I'll repeatedly emphasize that an effective leader must learn how to get subordinates to start solving their own problems, how to build a problem-solving team, how and when to enlist the creative resources of group members, and how to build relationships in which subordinates do not put distance between themselves and their leader. Unlike the goal of becoming omniscient, these goals *can* be achieved.

IV. SKILLS THAT HELP SUBORDINATES SOLVE THEIR PROBLEMS

WHEN your subordinates or group members encounter problems trying to get their various needs met, the overall effectiveness of your group must necessarily suffer. It goes almost without saying that when people are bothered or dissatisfied with something, it affects their work. Some may be distracted from concentrating; some spend excessive time ventilating their feelings or griping to other group members; others make mistakes and lose their motivation for high productivity; or they may drastically reduce communication with leaders or other members. Obviously, it helps leaders if they recognize the symptoms of subordinate problems—both personal and job-related—as early as possible so they may take steps to help them solve the problems and get back to productive work.

As everyone also knows, all people don't share their problems with others freely and openly. Sometimes, because we're not aware of what's bothering us, openly articulating our feelings can be difficult. Admitting to others that we are experiencing a problem may not be easy because of fear we'll be judged and evaluated negatively or subjected to irritation or anger. These inhibitors are particularly strong if the other person is *boss*. Group members' problems therefore are usually not communicated to leaders right away—and often not at all.

Even when subordinates muster the courage to share problems with a superior, they usually don't send messages that are crystal clear. Nevertheless, when people harbor an unmet need or a dissatisfaction, you can spot certain telltale cues and clues, such as:

Being unusually uncommunicative

Sulking

Avoiding you

Excessive absenteeism

Being unusually irritable

Not smiling as much as usual

Daydreaming

Tardiness

Looking downcast or depressed

Being sarcastic

Walking slower (or faster)

Slouching in their chairs

Such cues and clues alert you to the *existence* of a problem, but they seldom tell you the *nature* of the problem. This more difficult task lies ahead—getting the people to identify their problem. Even those who are unusually open and direct seldom identify the content of a problem immediately. As a rule, people don't get down to the *real* problem until after they have first ventilated a feeling or sent some opening message, such as:

"I'm really upset."

"Should have stayed in bed today."

"That damn purchasing department is driving me nuts."

"Oh, forget it."

"Mother told me there would be days like this."

"Get off my back, will you!"

"If it isn't one thing, it's another."

"How do you expect me to do my job without adequate information?"

"I cannot stand the way Shirley acts in our meetings!"

"I feel like quitting sometime."

It is important to understand that one never *knows* exactly what another person is experiencing, because it is impossible to be inside the other person's skin. All you can do is *guess* what is going on inside another, relying on interpretation of the messages you hear, whether verbal or nonverbal. This process of understanding another consists of several events. It starts out with the sender experiencing a feeling—some kind of dissatisfaction, internal disequilibrium, or deprivation:

SENDER   RECEIVER

The receiver can't possibly know what is in the sender's "private world of meaning," but if the sender wants to share it he must first select an appropriate *code* that will represent or symbolize the inner feelings:

SENDER   RECEIVER

Next, the sender transmits that code (in this case a verbal message):

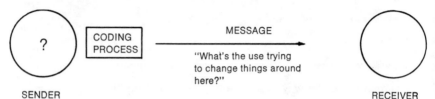

When you hear this particular code, you, the receiver, must start a *decoding* process: you guess or infer from the message what the sender is experiencing internally. Say your guess in this case is that the sender is feeling very discouraged:

This diagram of the interpersonal communication process is a visual way of showing that communication is more than someone expressing something, as people generally think. In actuality it requires the *expression* of a sender and the *impression* of a receiver. Effective or completed communication, then, only occurs when

IMPRESSION = EXPRESSION

Real understanding of another person happens only when the receiver's impression (the results of decoding) matches closely what the sender intended in his or her expression.

Unfortunately, effective communication with real understanding is much rarer than most people think because:

People don't always feel free to say what they really mean.

People are not always in touch with their real feelings.

Feelings are somewhat hard to put into words (it's hard to find the right code).

The same words (codes) have different meanings for different people.

We sometimes hear only what we want to hear (we decode selectively).

Receivers are often so busy thinking up what they're going to say next that they don't even bother to decode the sender's message (so they fail to understand).

The sender may not know whether the receiver has decoded correctly.

The receiver may not be certain that he has decoded correctly.

While these difficulties make real understanding hard to achieve, we have recently learned a great deal about how to increase the chances that IMPRESSION = EXPRESSION. And we also know rather precisely what acts as barriers.

First, a reminder: we are dealing with how people *initially* express themselves when they have a problem—with cues and clues or brief opening feeling messages. They're still a long way from starting the *problem-solving process.* A leader's task is to try to get that process into motion and to be skillful in facilitating the subordinate's carrying the process through the six separate steps of problem-solving:

I.   Identifying and defining the problem

II. Generating alternative solutions

III. Evaluating the alternative solutions

IV. Decision-making

V. Implementing the decision

VI. Following up to evaluate the solution

Again: the leader's goal is to "see to it that the problem gets solved."

RESPONSES THAT FACILITATE PROBLEM-SOLVING

Door Openers

After a person sends a brief opening feeling message, which clues the listener to the possible existence of a problem, the "helpee" usually will not move into the problem-solving process unless the listener sends an invitation—opens the door for the helpee:

"Would you like to talk about it?"

"Can I be of any help with this problem?"

"I'd be interested to hear how you feel."

"Would it help to talk about it?"

"Sometimes it helps to get it off your chest."

"I'd sure like to help if I can."

"Tell me about it."

"I've got the time if you have. Want to talk?"

Generally, people with problems are afraid of imposing them on others—taking up their time, "burdening" them, "unloading" on them, and so on. They usually need some kind of assurance of the willingness of the listener to assume the role of helper. These responses show much more tangibly that the listener is "with" the sender, not only hearing but also taking it in. Good listeners demonstrate close attention.

Passive Listening

As everyone knows from experience, when you have a problem and find someone who shuts up and listens, you are usually encouraged to keep talking about your problem. The listener's willingness to keep quiet is usually understood as reasonable evidence of interest and concern. Silence (or passive listening) is a potent tool for getting people to talk about what's bothering them; and, as anyone knows who has received counseling from a professional counselor, talking to someone who is willing to listen may be just the encouragement a person needs to keep going.

Acknowledgment Responses

Most people with a problem on their minds need something more from a listener than complete silence. They would like evidence that the listener is not woolgathering or engaged in his or her own thoughts. They need occasional acknowledgments of their messages, such as:

Eye contact	"Interesting."
Nodding	"Really."
"I see."	"No fooling."
"Oh."	"Yeah."
"Mm-hmm."	"I hear you."
"I understand."	

Active Listening

While Door Openers, Passive Listening, and Acknowledgment Responses help people start talking, they do not contribute much to ensuring that

$$IMPRESSION = EXPRESSION$$

None of the three techniques assures the helpee that the listener actually *understands*. To be sure that the listener's impression matches the helpee's expression, the listener must use a more active kind of listening.

Let me go back to my last diagram, in which the sender selected the message, "What's the use of trying to change things around here?" The receiver decoded this message as, "He is feeling very discouraged." Now, suppose the receiver feeds back exactly how that particular message got decoded:

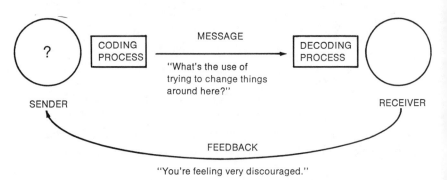

"You're feeling very discouraged."

From such a feedback the sender gets *tangible* evidence how the receiver decoded the message. And after hearing the feedback, the sender can either confirm it ("That's right") or correct it ("I'm more angry than I am discouraged"). The sender's *confirmation* would be proof to the listener of the accuracy of his or her "impression." His *correction* would reveal its inaccuracy.

Frequent and continuous feedback of the results of the receiver's decoding is what "Active Listening" is all about. We can never be absolutely certain we have completely or accurately understood another person, so it is essential to test the accuracy of our listening and minimize the misunderstanding and distortion that occur in most interpersonal communication. Door Openers, Passive Listening, and Acknowledgment Responses show only the listener's *intent* to understand; Active Listening gives proof that the listener has indeed understood. This proof is what makes the sender keep talking and go deeper into the problem.

Active Listening is certainly not complex. Listeners need only restate, in their own language, their impression of the expression of the sender. It's a check: is my impression acceptable to the sender? Still, learning to do Active Listening well is a rather difficult task requiring a lot of practice over a period of time. Experience from training thousands of leaders in my Leader Effectiveness Training (L.E.T.) course confirms that most trainees can acquire a reasonable level of competence in several weeks.

To get more familiar with this way of responding, first read each of the following messages and then read aloud the listener's response (each is an accurate feedback):

1. Sender: I don't know how I'm going to untangle this messy problem.
   Listener: You're really stumped on how to solve this one.

2. Sender: Damn it! Why can't I get accurate blueprints out of Engineering?
   Listener: It makes you angry when you find errors in their prints.

3. Sender: I'm sorry, I wasn't listening to you. I guess my mind is occupied with a problem at home with my son, Gregg. He's all screwed up.
   Listener: Sounds like you're really worried about Gregg.

4. Sender: Please, don't ask me about that now.
   Listener: Sounds like you're awfully busy right now.

5. Sender: I thought the meeting today accomplished nothing!
   Listener: You were very disappointed with our session.

6. Sender: I don't see why the hell I have to fill out two pages of that form every time I want something from Purchasing.

   Listener: You're finding it too time-consuming and question its usefulness, I gather.

THE RATIONALE FOR ACTIVE LISTENING

To prevent or minimize misunderstandings in person-to-person communication would be sufficient reason for leaders to make the effort to become competent Active Listeners. But other reasons are equally compelling.

For the last three or four decades some psychologists have been attempting to identify the critical ingredients in human relationships that foster personal growth and psychological health. This intensive search, which initially focused only on identifying the characteristics and behavior of effective professional helping agents (counselors and psychotherapists), eventually led some to study the personal qualities of effective teachers, effective marriage partners, and effective parents. Rather conclusive evidence emerged that at least two ingredients are necessary in any relationship of one person fostering growth and psychological health in another—*empathy* and *acceptance.*

Empathy is the capacity to put oneself in the shoes of others and understand their "personal world of meaning" —how they view their reality, how they feel about things. Active Listening performs this very function. A climate in which a person can frequently feel empathically understood is conducive to that person's overall psychological health and personal growth. I believe this happens primarily because such a climate *facilitates problem-solving,* which results in greater need satisfaction. When people solve problems and get their needs satisfied, they are freed to move farther up Maslow's pyramid toward

the higher level needs, discovering new
ing self-achievement and self-development.
Acceptance, you will recall, is feeling good ab
a person is doing, and "Acceptable Behaviors" be
the top area of the behavioral rectangle:

```
┌──────────────────┐
│                  │
│    Acceptable    │
│    Behaviors     │
│                  │
├──────────────────┤
│                  │
│   Unacceptable   │
│    Behaviors     │
│                  │
└──────────────────┘
```

Obviously we have no need to change acceptable behaviors, and so we can accept the other person just as he or
she is at the moment (the behavior is not interfering with
our own needs getting met). Passive Listening, Acknowledgment Responses, and *particularly* Active Listening
are the verbal responses (or vehicles) for communicating
acceptance because they communicate clearly:

I hear what you are feeling.

I understand how you are seeing things now.

I see you as you are right now.

I am interested and concerned.

I understand where you are now.

I have no desire to change you.

I do not judge or evaluate you.

You don't have to feel afraid of my censure.

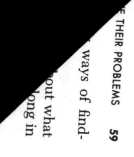

sive Listening, Acknowledg-
Listening, certain other mes-
the listener's desire or intent
d to direct his or her behavior
behave differently. These re-
bit problem-solving, which is
Roadblocks." There are 12 of
examples:

anding

You must do this.

You cannot do this.

I expect you to do this.

Stop it.

Go apologize to her.

2. *Warning, Admonishing, Threatening*

You had better do this, or else . . .

If you don't do this, then . . .

You better not try that.

I warn you, if you do that . . .

3. *Moralizing, Preaching, Imploring*

You should do this.

You ought to try it.

It is your responsibility to do this.

It is your duty to do this.

I wish you would do this.

I urge you to do this.

4. *Advising, Giving Suggestions or Solutions*

What I think you should do is . . .

Let me suggest . . .

It would be best for you if . . .

Why not take a different approach?

The best solution is . . .

5. *Persuading with Logic, Lecturing, Arguing*

Do you realize that . . .

The facts are in favor of . . .

Let me give you the facts.

Here is the right way.

Experience tells us that . . .

6. *Judging, Criticizing, Disagreeing, Blaming*

You are acting foolishly.

You are not thinking straight.

You are out of line.

You didn't do it right.

You are wrong.

That is a stupid thing to say.

7. *Praising, Agreeing, Evaluating Positively, Buttering Up*

You usually have very good judgment.

You are an intelligent person.

You have so much potential.

You've made quite a bit of progress.

You have always made it in the past.

8. *Name-calling, Ridiculing, Shaming*

You are a sloppy worker.

You are a fuzzy thinker.

You're talking like an engineer.

You really goofed on this one!

9. *Interpreting, Analyzing, Diagnosing*

   You're saying this because you're angry.

   You are jealous.

   What you really need is . . .

   You have problems with authority.

   You want to look good.

   You are being a bit paranoid.

10. *Reassuring, Sympathizing, Consoling, Supporting*

    You'll feel different tomorrow.

    Things will get better.

    It is always darkest before the dawn.

    Behind every cloud there's a silver lining.

    Don't worry so much about it.

    It's not that bad.

11. *Probing, Questioning, Interrogating*

    Why did you do that?

    How long have you felt this way?

    What have you done to try to solve it?

    Have you consulted with anyone?

    When did you become aware of this feeling?

    Who has influenced you?

12. *Distracting, Diverting, Kidding*

    Think about the positive side.

    Try not to think about it until you're rested.

    Let's have lunch and forget about it.

    That reminds me of the time when . . .

    You think you've got problems!

Implicit (and sometimes quite explicit) in these 12 categories of listener responses is the desire or intent to *change* rather than accept the sender. The Roadblocks communicate a desire for (and often pressure for) the helpee to think, feel, or behave differently. These 12 types of responses, then, act as *vehicles for communicating unacceptance*. And we know that a climate of unacceptance is very unconducive to personal growth, development, and psychological health.

Why? It seems that people don't problem-solve very effectively when they fear arbitrary power to make them change, or when they feel threatened, judged, put down, or analyzed so they will change. Such a climate produces defensiveness and resistance to change (the person protects Level II safety and security needs); it also inhibits self-expression and self-exploration—both necessary for solving one's problems.

Listening performs another very important function in helping subordinates solve their problems—it helps keep the responsibility for problem-solving with the subordinate (who, of course, is the one who "owns the problem"). The 12 Roadblocks, on the other hand, in varying degrees, tend to grab that responsibility away from the owner of the problem and deposit it in the hands of the leader.

Keeping the "locus of responsibility" in the one who owns the problem is important because:

First, leaders who get subordinates to solve their own problems are making a sound investment that will pay off with many benefits: their subordinates will become less dependent on their leaders, more self-directing, more self-sufficient, and more capable of solving problems on their own.

Second, leaders seldom have enough understanding of the complexities and wide variety of personal problems which group members encounter in their lives, on the job and off. Consequently, skills that keep the locus of responsibility for problem-solving with the helpee relieve leaders of the impossible task of coming up with answers to problems about which they have little information. Even highly trained professional counselors, recognizing how limited their understanding of another's problem usually is, refrain from assuming responsibility for generating solutions for their clients, often despite heavy pressure to do so.

Here is an actual dialogue between a foreman and his superintendent. Note how the foreman tries to shift responsibility to his superior:

Foreman: Well, I have a problem out here—my men have come to me today and asked me how come they don't get any overtime when the guys over in X's department are coming in on Saturdays and getting in on some of the gravy.

Supt.: Your men wish they could get some overtime?

Foreman: Yeah—well, it's not too much that. I want to hold the costs down in my department and I don't have any overtime for these fellows, but naturally they're going to squawk for overtime if X is going to bring his men in—now that's only natural, don't you think?

Supt.: You don't want to bring your men in, but it puts you in a spot if X's men come in and get overtime.

Foreman: Sure, and maybe it's none of my business, but I'd just like to cite this fact. He has got a bunch of duds there, and one good man could do what three of those bums do in a day, and that's why he's got to bring those guys in on Saturday to get caught up on his work.

Supt.: I see—you feel that if he didn't have those duds but had some good men on those jobs, he wouldn't have to work anyone overtime. Have you been able to express your feelings about this to X?

Foreman: Oh, hell no, what's the use! Well, now let me ask you, don't you think I am right?

The superintendent later commented on this conversation and explained his reasons for refusing to take the responsibility away from this subordinate:

"In this case there was a mixture of conditions. This foreman was getting reactions from his men that were causing him difficulty. On the other hand, he had judgments about the policies and performance of his coforeman. Yet he could not face the other foreman directly; he insisted it was my job to do that. I told him that I realized his problem with his own men was acute, that I could convey his problem to the other foreman but not his judgments about the poor workers in the other department. I also said that I was reluctant to carry this communication and hoped we might someday reach a point where each man felt free to carry his feelings directly to the others involved. I really didn't know whether his judgments were justified, and I said so. However, I indicated a willingness to sit in with both of them to discuss it. The foreman declined this offer."

Here is another situation. A plant manager in an Iowa manufacturing organization, trained in Active Listening, persistently kept the locus of responsibility with his subordinate. Result: the foreman solved his own problem.

"One day a foreman came into the office and closed the door carefully behind him. He said he had a grave problem and wanted to talk it over. He explained that he shared a material bin with another foreman, and couldn't get along without the material in this bin. However, the other foreman had forbidden him to use it.

"He explained that he wanted to figure out carefully what to do, and wanted me to think carefully with him. He said: 'Now I want to do the right thing here. I realize what's going on. I know that Ev has it against me. This has been going on for a long time. Damn it, I've got nothing against the guy, but I know how he feels about me, and he's bucking me all down the line, and yet

I can understand why he feels that way because it goes way back, and there ain't nothing going to change the way he's feeling. And even so, I've still got a job to get done for myself, and him feeling the way he does, it makes it damn tough for me to operate. So all I want to do is figure out real careful the best thing to do because I know he ain't going to change his tactics and all I want to do is just go my way and get my job done.'

"An hour-long discussion ensued. The foreman talked and I concentrated on understanding his feelings and trying to follow him as he dove deeper into them. Most of his time was spent explaining past incidents of poor relations he had had with his coforeman, and trying to evaluate the other foreman's behavior. I neither condoned nor rejected his judgment of the other foreman. When the discussion ended, he had identified for himself what he felt the problem to be, and had decided on a course of action.

"I felt my role here was one of hands-off in the friction between these two men. I had heard from each of them, and each had gradually revealed some deep feelings. However, it seemed more useful for me to provide a place where they could safely work through their own problems, rather than to put myself into the picture to 'create harmony' or 'fix things up' or 'straighten these fellows out.' I believed I was doing both men more good by leaving their relationship up to them, and to time, to heal. I felt confident that they would work their problem out together.

"Several weeks later I asked the foreman who had come to me with the problem how he was making out. He grinned and said: 'Oh, we've got it all worked out. I figured out how to talk to him, and put it up to him. You've got to be scientific on these things.' "

The amazing effectiveness of Active Listening in keeping responsibility entirely with the problem owner (and at the same time be a catalyst to help the person work through the problem-solving process toward finding her own solution) comes through in the following dialogue between a supervisor and one of her subordinates:

Kate: Do you have a few minutes to give me some help on a problem, Nancy?

Nancy: Sure, Kate. I have a half hour before a meeting. Is that enough?

Kate: Oh, plenty. It's not a very complicated problem, but it's sure beginning to bother me.

Nancy: You're really beginning to feel bugged by it, huh?

Kate: Yeah. No fooling. I've got a woman working for me that puzzles the hell out of me. I just can't figure her out. I thought maybe you might know what to do with this kind of character.

Nancy: Sounds like you're really stumped.

Kate: Yeah. Never saw anyone quite like her. Well, let's see—how to describe her. First, she's damned bright—no question about that. She's got a brain and all that, but she sure knows it. The trouble is, she thinks she has the answer to everything. If I make a suggestion to her, she always finds something wrong with it—some reason why it won't work.

Nancy: It frustrates you when she resists everything you suggest.

Kate: Boy, does it! Then she usually comes up with two or three ideas that she thinks are better ones, but her ideas are so kookie—almost every time what she suggests is something real different from what we're doing. Or they're ideas that would require us to change our methods or work up some new gadget or take time to develop a new form or something like that.

Nancy: You see her ideas as too novel or too unique—or maybe you're saying they would require too much deviation from what you're used to doing in your department.

Kate: Well, I don't mind constructive suggestions occasionally. But she gives me the feeling—every damned day—that our way of doing things is outmoded or old-fashioned! Like we're not progressive or modern or something like that.

Nancy: You don't like being made to feel you're behind the times.

Kate: Hell, no! These young gals with their college education get the idea that they know everything—that everything has to be changed. I get tired of hearing that all the time! Like experience doesn't count for anything.

Nancy: You hate to hear your experience devalued, and you get fed up with her trying to pressure you to change things.

Kate: I sure do! I've got to admit that some of her ideas are not bad. She's smart, all right. I just wish I knew how to get her to appreciate my long experience in this work and not assume that everything we do is wrong.

Nancy: You really value some of her ideas, but you want her to appreciate you.

Kate: I don't really need appreciation. We've got our share of problems, but what department doesn't? There just isn't time to deal with all of them.

Nancy: You're aware of where improvements could be made, but you feel you can't find the time to tackle all those problems.

Kate: That's right. I guess we could schedule a special meeting some night after work.

Nancy: That's a possibility, huh.

Kate: Yeah. Then I wouldn't be the only one who has to defend a lot of the things we're doing to this eager beaver. Others in the group might convince her.

Nancy: You'd like to have others help you, and get the monkey off your back.

Kate: I sure would. And we might also make a few changes, which would be OK with me.

Nancy: You're thinking that a meeting might kill two birds with one stone.

Kate: Yes, I think so. We need to get together as a group more. I'm going to schedule one next week. The earlier the better.

Nancy: It's such a good idea, you want to move fast on this.

Kate: Yeah. I should be getting back to work now—I've got to work out some solution to that mix-up we discovered with our back orders. Thanks for hearing me out, Nancy.

Nancy: You're welcome, Kate.

Did you notice that never once did Nancy take the ball away from Kate? She listened empathically, she used feedback after each of Kate's messages, and she avoided using any of the Roadblocks. Kate's lack of defensiveness was apparent, enabling her to come up with a solution that pleased her.

ACTIVE LISTENING IN ITS PROPER PERSPECTIVE

So far, my illustrations of Active Listening have been carefully selected, principally to help you learn to recognize exactly what kind of a response it is, how it differs from the twelve Roadblocks, and how it sounds in a dialogue between two people, one of whom has a problem. To prevent misunderstandings and misconceptions, much more must be said about this important skill.

Do I Need to Feedback Every Message?

Of course not. Remember there are three other kinds of responses that facilitate problem-solving: Door Openers, Passive Listening, and Acknowledgment Responses. You'll find yourself using these, too, when you try to be an effective counselor to a person with a problem. Also, there will be times when you won't understand certain messages well enough to feedback—you'll have to respond with silence or a few "Mm-hmm's."

Can't I Ever Use the Roadblocks?

Certainly, but generally not when it is the other person's problem. The four helping responses are best when the sender *owns a problem* and asks for your help in working it through. At these special times, the Roadblocks have a *very high probability* of blocking further communication from the helpee and inhibiting his or her problem-solving. At other times, as I'll show later, the Roadblocks have a *low probability* of blocking communication—for example, in the No-problem Area or productive work time. At these times, it'll seldom hurt your relationships with group members when you give directions, instruct, advise, offer solutions, ask questions, evaluate, or even kid. Even then, however, it is essential that you stay sensitive and recognize cues and clues signaling that a group member is no longer problem-free and productive. This is when you should shift immediately to Active Listening.

Can I Trust That Others Can Always Solve Their Problem?

This is the best assumption to make because we usually err on the side of underestimating people's ability to solve their own problems. Of course, people do not *always* come up with solutions to their problems. You'll discover times when you offer to help and start being a good listener, but the helpee doesn't feel like problem-solving at that particular moment. So you should back off and respect that. At other times you'll get a surprise when a problem owner does no more than state the problem and ventilate feelings and that is all that's needed apparently —no solution, just a little empathy from a listener, a chance to have your feelings accepted. There will be still other times when a helpee advances only through Step I and Step II of the problem-solving process, warmly thanks you for listening, and then leaves. Don't feel disappointed! Often they will later complete the problem-solving process without you, or perhaps seek you out later for further help. Finally, people often have problems whose solution requires resources (knowledge, tools, money) they do not possess, as in this example:

Member: I'm in a real bind. I need to purchase fifty five-dollar, three-ring binders, but I don't know if the department budget would allow me to make that expenditure.

Leader: Well, it is tight, but let me figure out whether we can find where that amount of money might have been allocated for something else. Can I get back to you?

We use the term "legitimate dependency" for such situations—those times when someone is legitimately dependent on you for information or for some other resource because you have what the helpee needs and doesn't have. In such cases, Active Listening is not only unnecessary; it's usually inappropriate.

Does Active Listening Imply Agreement?

It is understandable why this question is often asked—most of us are accustomed to communications that convey either agreement or disagreement. When people listen to people, they typically respond with words that connote right or wrong, sound or unsound, logical or illogical, good or bad. Active Listening never conveys negative evaluation or disagreement, yet on first exposure to this technique some leaders are afraid that feeding back a person's feelings (especially anger, hate, discouragement, hopelessness, and the like) might convey, "I think you're justified in your feelings," "I sanction your feelings," "I think you're right," or "I agree with you." Which is why I'm often asked, "Won't Active Listening reinforce or strengthen negative feelings?"

Such fears are based on mistaking *acceptance* for agreement. "You're really feeling hopeless" is quite different from "I agree that it's hopeless."

Active Listening communicates, "I hear what you're feeling," neither agreement nor disagreement, no judgment whether the feelings are right or wrong. The listener only conveys acceptance that the feelings exist. This kind of acceptance can be very disarming because people so seldom encounter it. This explains the unique effect of Active Listening—the sender is left with the sole responsibility for assessing the appropriateness or inappropriateness of the feelings, which in fact usually happens. And this often leads into productive problem-solving.

Are Listening Skills All I Need?

No, but they will suffice in many situations when your group members have problems that interfere with getting their needs met. At other times, it will be obvious to you, after you have understood a subordinate's problem, that you will have to take some definitive action to see to it that the problem gets solved.

Jean is unhappy because you have frequently let your staff meetings run on past quitting time, causing her to miss her ride home in the car pool.

Carl tells you his efficiency suffers because he doesn't have sufficient filing space and needs another three-drawer file cabinet in his office.

Mark is upset because he cannot get enough time from typists in the typing pool, causing costly delays in completing his projects.

Your group members convince you that their productivity is seriously reduced because of a company policy that requires unnecessary paper work. However, you can't change the policy without the approval of your superior.

Art asks you if he could take off an hour early twice a week so he can be home when his youngsters come from school. He offers to come an hour earlier each day.

Each of these problems obviously requires some action on your part. To Active Listen to the subordinates' problems would not be enough. They need answers, or they need you to intercede for them. While Active Listening might have facilitated getting the problem defined and generating a solution, that solution turned out to be something *you* have to do.

Being an understanding, empathic, and accepting listener is an essential skill for an effective leader, but it is not the only tool for solving the problems your group members will encounter.

What If I Don't Feel Like Listening?

Remember, while Active Listening is a powerful technique for helping people solve their own problems, it is still only a *vehicle*—a way of communicating your attitudes of acceptance and empathic understanding. If, for whatever reason, you don't feel accepting when a group member shares a problem, the Active Listening skill will never disguise your true feelings. And if it is not your intention to be understanding, you won't do an accurate job of listening anyway.

Suppose a group member wants to talk about a problem just when you are terribly busy doing something that must be completed immediately—finishing up a report your boss needs, making several important phone calls, rushing to a meeting you must attend. This is not the time to begin Active Listening—your heart won't be in it. Far better to tell the person that you are unable to help at that time, explain the reason, and ask if he or she would be willing to come back later when you'll feel like helping.

Recall how the "full cup principle" emphasizes that, unless you are relatively fulfilled (free from the press of your own needs), you will not be in the mood to be a helper to another. Nor will you be good at it. Helping another through the problem-solving steps takes not only time but also a genuine feeling of acceptance on your part. So don't pretend to be accepting if you're not, and don't offer to help if you don't feel like it. Most problems group members develop will wait a few hours (or a few days, even) until you feel like putting yourself in the helping role.

To listen to another person empathically and accurately requires intense attention, so you will find you cannot listen with the required concentration if you are engrossed in your own thoughts or worried about something. Group members don't need leaders who *always* listen; they do need leaders who listen when they can genuinely feel understanding, accepting, and caring.

V. MAKING EVERYDAY USE OF YOUR LISTENING SKILLS

SITUATIONS requiring the use of empathic listening are almost limitless in groups and organizations. It is no exaggeration to say that leaders have opportunities every day to put their listening skills to work. If you make the effort to acquire competence in this essential communications tool you'll be amply rewarded by many tangible results. But competence can only be acquired by working at it. As with any other skill, formal training that provides coaching from an instructor is obviously the best way to start learning Active Listening, but in the long run the responsibility for learning rests entirely with you, and improvement will come only from practice in a variety of situations. In this chapter I will show you just how you can employ your listening skill in everyday situations.

FEELINGS ARE FRIENDLY

People are conditioned almost from infancy to think of feelings as bad and dangerous—enemies of good human relationships. People grow up afraid of feelings—

their own and those of others around them—largely because they have heard from adults in their lives many messages like these:

"Don't ever let me hear you say you hate your baby brother."

"You shouldn't feel discouraged about what happened."

"If you can't say something pleasant, don't say anything at all."

"Don't feel bad about it—things will be better tomorrow."

"There's nothing at all to be afraid of."

"Keep a stiff upper lip."

"Swallow your pride."

"Hold your temper, young lady."

Later, we encounter additional reinforcement of the strong ban against expressing feelings—in the world of work, where we are warned that feelings simply do not belong. Somehow feelings and emotions are perceived as the antithesis of the rationality and shallowness required in relationships we want in the workplace. Leaving your worries at the doorstep and biting your tongue are the behaviors considered appropriate for people in organizations; people feel these behaviors will be valued and rewarded in the long run.

This pervasive and repressive group norm not only contributes heavily to poor psychological health; it is counterproductive to organizational effectiveness. As everyone knows very well, working with people inevitably generates feelings—of all kinds—ranging from mild to strong: irritation, anger, frustration, disappointment, hurt, fear, futility, despair, hate, bitterness, discouragement. While *experiencing* such feelings is not unhealthy, *repressing* them is. Continually bottling up your feelings is very definitely "hazardous to your health," and can ultimately cause ulcers, headaches, heartburn, high blood pressure, spastic colon, or any number of other psychosomatic problems. Repressed feelings can also reduce your effectiveness just by distracting you from your work.

Asked how he was able to stand the repressive climate of the school where he worked, a teacher once told me, "I use the three-martinis-before-dinner method like most of the teachers here." A division sales manager in another organization where I was as a consultant had this formula for survival: "I keep my mouth shut and my nose clean."

Contrary to the "feelings don't belong here" belief, there is evidence that expressing feelings actually increases a group's effectiveness and productivity. Openness in expressing feelings serves very much the same function for a group as pain does for one's organism. Pain is a warning signal that something is wrong inside one's body; feelings of group members are similar warning signals to leaders that something is wrong inside their group. Consequently, it pays the leader to foster a climate in which group members feel free to express their feelings.

Leaders should treat feelings as "friendly," not dangerous. Feelings should be welcomed because they are cues and clues that some problem exists. With this attitude, leaders will not ignore the signals or, worse yet, roadblock the senders of such messages. Instead they should encourage people through Active Listening to go beyond the feelings and get to the underlying problem. Contrast the two different ways of responding to feelings in the following hypothetical situations:

1. Member: Holy cow! Not another bitch about what we're doing in the shop!
   (a) Leader: Come on, Fred, accept it as constructive criticism (MORALIZING, PREACHING).
   (b) Leader: Sounds like you feel you're getting it from all sides (ACTIVE LISTENING).

2. Member: Why the hell does Madge make so damned many mistakes?

   (a) Leader: She's under a lot of pressure these days (LECTURING, GIVING FACTS).

   (b) Leader: You're feeling really upset with her performance (ACTIVE LISTENING).

3. Member: I don't feel very confident about my ability to tackle that job.

   (a) Leader: I know you can do it if you try (REASSURING).

   (b) Leader: You're afraid it's going to be too much for you (ACTIVE LISTENING).

4. Member: You won't catch me sticking my neck out again in staff meetings.

   (a) Leader: Jim, you were off base, obviously (JUDGING, CRITICIZING).

   (b) Leader: You're sorry you spoke up and perhaps your feelings were hurt (ACTIVE LISTENING).

In each of these examples, it's highly probable that the first response to the group member's feeling will block movement toward problem identification. The second responses, all Active Listening, more likely will convey acceptance and encourage the group member to go beyond the feeling and into defining the real problem.

FEELINGS CAN BE TRANSITORY

When someone says, "I hate this job!" or "I can't work with Betty!" or "Nobody values my work around here!" most people are inclined to think that those feelings are rather permanent and unchangeable. And, usually, the stronger the feeling, the more it sounds final or irreversible. For example, if my wife should greet me at the door with, "I'm so damned mad at you!" my immediate reaction would be that I've fouled my nest somehow and she'll never feel the same about me again. Parents, too, have a similar reaction when one of their youngsters blurts out, "I'm never going to go anyplace with you again, never!"

Fortunately, negative feelings can be quite transitory. One of the reasons for this is that people purposely select strong negative feelings as *codes* to communicate "I want to make sure I get your full attention" or "I want you to know how bad you've made me feel." If the receiver is able to decode the negative feeling and respond with acceptance and empathic understanding, almost like magic the strong feeling disappears and gets replaced by a much less intense feeling—even by a positive feeling. I have often heard a small child tell a parent, "I hate you" or "You're a terrible parent," but in less than a minute, provided the parent accepts the first feeling, the child ends up hugging and kissing the parent.

The same thing happens with adult relationships in groups and organizations. When leaders recognize that strong feelings are not carved in granite, they become much less frightened by them and more able to deal with them constructively. Again, Active Listening is the best tool, for it usually has the effect of defusing the feeling. This is illustrated in the following excerpt from an interview we conducted with the industrial relations director of a midwestern chemical company:

"I want to tell you about an instance where the president of the union had come into my office extremely upset. He was so wrapped up in his feelings I wasn't having any influence at all. I gave him answers to the questions he asked and that upset him even more—to the point he got up and started walking out of my office. With his back about two steps out of my office, I raised my voice slightly and said, 'You really are upset about this thing.' And he stopped, hesitated, turned around, and his face was beet red at that point. But he came back, sat down, and said,

'You're damned right I am!' And he laid it out—he was in my office for five more minutes. When he left, although we still had some significant problems, the shade of red was about half of what it had been before. And I didn't have the feeling he was going to charge out of there and start stirring up a lot of trouble for us. The thing had been defused slightly. I think he was hoping something would happen that would avoid his having to take the actions he was threatening."

The next time someone sends you an emotion-packed message, sit back and Active Listen to demonstrate your understanding and acceptance of that person's feeling. It might just go away as suddenly as it erupted.

GETTING TO THE REAL PROBLEM

People's problems are like onions—they come in layers. Only after the outside layers are peeled off do they get down to the core problem. Sometimes people know what the real problem is but are afraid to start there; more often they are not even aware of what is underneath. When a person starts out talking to you about some bothersome problem, you generally hear only the "presenting problem." Active Listening effectively facilitates the helpee to move through the presenting problem and finally get down to the core problem.

A supervisor we interviewed months after he took the L.E.T. course described how he had learned to wait and listen until his subordinates got to their real problems:

"For years I've felt one of my problems was when you'd be talking to me I wouldn't listen. I've learned to listen—not try and think ahead of how I'm going to answer you. I've done that a lot. If a guy came in bitching to me about something, right away I start thinking how am I going to answer this monkey. I mean, not listening to him at all. So I've gained a lot. Now when a guy comes in with a problem, I have to just block out my thoughts and I'll listen and take notes sometimes. What happened was that what I found myself doing is I would sometimes solve the wrong problem—I'd have the answers before he was halfway through. It would be an answer but not the answer to the problem that's really bugging him."

Here is another person using Active Listening to help an employee move from a presenting problem to the more basic one:

The personnel counselor for the administrative offices of a western city told how Active Listening had enabled her to find out the real problem in a conference with one of the city employees. At first the employee complained bitterly about the unfairness of a performance appraisal she had just received from her manager. The personnel counselor was certain the employee felt that the work objectives that her boss had set were unfair and unattainable. Active Listening finally uncovered the real problem: the employee had already decided to resign because she was getting married and moving away to Vancouver, so she was afraid she could not get a good letter of recommendation from the company to take to her next job. When the real problem surfaced, the personnel counselor helped the employee make a decision to approach her manager directly and ask for the reference letter. Actually, she ended up getting a good recommendation.

In this situation, as so often happens, a little bit of listening to the presenting problem uncovered the employee's deeper concern, for which an appropriate solution was worked out.

PEOPLE ARE MORE LIKABLE THAN YOU THINK

Everyone evaluates and judges, although in varying degrees. When we see people behaving in certain ways we tend to form judgments about what they are like and how much we like them. When we fail to understand what is behind people's behavior, especially if it is unusual, we are more likely to dislike them. Conversely, getting to know people usually makes us like them better. And, since Active Listening is such an effective way to encourage people to talk about themselves and their feelings, it is not surprising that one of the most common effects of Active Listening is that the listener discovers people are more likable than the listener previously thought.

Read the following excerpt from an interview with a supervisor who had recently completed the L.E.T. course. He sums it all up when he concludes, "Before, I wouldn't have given you a dime for him":

"I got this one guy who's now in the hospital but coming back to work soon. He was a guy a lot of people had trouble with, and I ended up getting him. I was told, 'All right, Gary, you got this guy, see what you can do with him.' At the beginning I personally could not get along with him. I didn't like him. But after I got to know the guy by listening to him and hearing what he had to say, we get along great now—no problem with him at all. Occasionally he goes off the deep end, and he'll come in and say, 'I wouldn't work no more overtime in this place for love or money.' And I calm him down and I talk with him and say, 'Now wait a minute, Bob, what's the problem?' He'll tell me and I listen and explain what's happened, and the next day he's fine. So I really think the L.E.T. course was good in this respect. I also find myself listening more at home with my family. Even Dr. ——— said, 'Gary has done more with Bob than anybody has.' I'll be honest with you—before I thought the guy should have been on a funny farm. But I found out what was causing his uproars. And, gee, we get along great together now. Before I wouldn't have given you a dime for him."

POURING OIL ON TROUBLED WATERS

When conflicts arise in human relationships, emotions often reach a high level and angry feelings are exchanged. During this stage, no one is in the proper mood for constructive problem-solving; they're too wrapped up in feeling and can't do the kind of thinking required for effective problem-solving. This is where Active Listening is very useful—helping people get their feelings off their chest, paving the way for subsequent problem-solving.

When people are angry or upset, they want it to be known—as if to say, "You must understand how very angry or upset I am before I'm willing to try to solve the problem that made me upset." Often people want to punish: "Look how angry or upset you've made me! Now aren't you sorry?" Still another reason why people ventilate strong feelings in a conflict is to scare the other person into meeting all their demands: "If I show enough anger and yell loud enough, maybe I'll get what I want." This is not unlike a child's temper tantrum, and, as parents know full well, the best strategy is to wait for the feelings to dissipate.

The following incident, related by a personnel director, illustrates how Active Listening can quiet down angry people and pave the way for problem-solving:

"The time it really worked well for me was with the union officers. Their previous style was to come charging in with some complaint, big or little, and make a big thing out of it. If they yelled loud enough, someone in management would give in and try to come up with some marshmallow for them so they would quiet down. After twenty years of that, we were at a point where we'd given away a large percent of what you had to start with. Well, after the L.E.T. I'd get out a pad of paper and say, 'You guys are really upset, but if you'll slow down a bit, I'll write it down here.' Those meetings had a typical turn—they went on for a period of time with them ranting and raving. And I'd be writing things down and Active Listening back whenever they would say, 'Such and such foreman in Plant 5 is doing awful stuff and we're going to have to retaliate with such and such.' And I'd keep feeding back that they were really upset and I wanted to find out more about it so we could determine if something might be done about it. They would usually quiet down, like it was pouring oil on water, they'd quiet down. And before the meeting was over, they would be very amenable and say things like, 'OK, we realize that there are problems here that need to be checked out. When can you give us an answer?' Invariably when they would come back it was on a totally different emotional level, such as 'Have you found out about such and such?' And I'd say, 'Yeah, here's what I found out.' My answers weren't always positive, and they didn't always hear what they wanted to hear, but even when they didn't, they still seemed appeased with the whole situation, feeling like they'd really been heard."

When people's emotions run high, as with these union representatives, I know of no better tool than Active Listening to get them to the point where "they are feeling like they'd really been heard."

HELPING YOUR PEOPLE GROW

Sometimes, though not often, an opportunity presents itself to a leader to contribute significantly to the personal growth of a group member. Without the Active Listening skill, leaders are certain to miss these opportunities to serve as counselors for a troubled subordinate. Unskilled leaders block the flow of communication with the Roadblocks and miss the chance to help subordinates work through a problem and develop new insights or reach constructive solutions. Leaders with skill in Active Listening can usually help subordinates turn problems into occasions for personal development.

Frequently, these counseling sessions with subordinates bring about significant improvements in their on-the-job performance: a shy person is helped to speak up more frequently in meetings; a worker gets insight into the causes of his or her carelessness and takes remedial action; an authoritarian supervisor is helped to understand his bossiness and begins to treat his workers more understandingly; a slow reader works through her fear of schooling and decides to enroll in a rapid reading course; a compulsive and perfectionistic bookkeeper relaxes her unrealistic standards and speeds up her performance, as in the following incident:

Hal: Cathy, I was really unhappy about the way our talk earlier today went—about your feelings, about your work load. I don't feel like the matter is resolved and I'd like to take another try at seeing if we can work this out. Would you be willing to tell me about your problem again?

Cathy: Sure, I was unhappy with the outcome, too. I felt you never really did understand how seriously I felt about that problem.

Hal: You were really upset, and I didn't act like I realized it, huh?

Cathy: That's right, because what I was saying to you, Hal, is that it's really affecting my work.

Hal: Uh-huh.

Cathy: I don't like this feeling that I'm behind and not really pulling my weight.

Hal: (Silence.)

Cathy: It makes me feel guilty and makes me feel bad when I go home at night.

Hal: So this is really getting to you?

Cathy: It really is, and I'd like to do something about it. (Pause.)

Hal: I see.

Cathy: I do know, Hal, that I am conscientious. I like to do good and accurate work.

Hal: Mm-hm.

Cathy: Sometimes I even think maybe I'm too conscientious, and I'm too much a stickler for accuracy.

Hal: Sounds like you're proud of your work and want to make it absolutely top-notch, but you're beginning to wonder if you're putting in too much time and effort on making it super-terrific.

Cathy: Yeah, I think so. There're times when I go over my figures three or four times, when down deep inside I know that's unnecessary, because I seldom find a mistake.

Hal: (Silence.)

Cathy: Sometimes I wish, well, I'd go over it once and push it aside and take on the next job. But there's something in me that says, well, I'd better do it again, because I don't want anybody catching me making a mistake.

Hal: Well, it sounds like you're really realizing that you overdo your checking, but something inside of you . . . some fear of getting caught in a mistake . . . just compels you to keep on checking.

Cathy: Yeah, I've always been that way. Not just about my work, but I'm that way about lots of things.

Hal: I see.

Cathy: I don't like people to catch me in mistakes. I guess you might say I'm kind of a perfectionist.

Hal: So you're seeing this as kind of a theme throughout your whole life. That you just have to be free of blame and perfect all the time.

Cathy: Yeah, but it's often a real burden because it takes time to be perfect. And it's as if sometimes I'm cutting my nose off to spite my face because I miss out on doing a lot of things, because I feel I shouldn't do them unless I do them perfectly.

Hal: So, this desire to be perfect is really preventing you from doing more things and having a richer life.

Cathy: Yeah, I'm beginning to see that that's true. For a long time, I've really wanted to play tennis, and two months ago I signed up for lessons.

Hal: No kidding.

Cathy: And my friends call me up to ask me to play, and I really like to play, but I say, no, I don't want to play.

Hal: Oh.

Cathy: The reason I say that is because I want to get more lessons so that I'll have more confidence.

Hal: I understand.

Cathy: So that when I do go play with my friends, they don't see that I make mistakes, or I guess I want them to see how good I am.

Hal: Uh . . . it almost sounds like you're seeing this . . . this need to look good is preventing you from making social contacts and having fun, and being free, and it's cutting out a lot of fun in life.

Cathy: That's right. Going back to my work, if I could get less compulsive about having to have everything perfect, I'm sure I'd get more done.

Hal: You almost sound like you have an idea for a solution to part of your problem, and that is to cut down on some of your worrying and checking. You're going to see how it goes.

Cathy: Yeah, because there're some things that just aren't worth three or four checks. There might be one mistake, that really isn't catastrophic, I think, in our business.
(Pause.)

Hal: I get it.

Cathy: In bookkeeping, there's so many cross checks that take place it isn't necessary for me to go over every column of figures . . . over and over again.

Hal: I see.

Cathy: I just think it has slowed me down.

Hal: So you can see there really wouldn't be as much of a penalty involved, if you let a mistake slip by every six months, as you've been imagining.

Cathy: Right, right, exactly!

Hal: That sounds like you're kind of working up your courage to test out that hypothesis.

Cathy: I'd like to give it a try for a week and see whether I can make this change. I'm not sure I can, but it makes so much sense to me, I'd like to give it a try, and get back to you if some other solution needs to be worked out.

Hal: Uh-huh.

Cathy: But I have a sneaking suspicion that this may really reduce that heavy work load I have on my desk . . . considerably.

Hal: So you're a little tentative about how it's going to come out, but you're willing to give it a try.

Cathy: Yes, I am.
         (Pause.)

Cathy: OK, I think I'll go back and give it a try. Thanks for listening.

Hal: You're sure welcome, and I feel real good about this conversation.

Cathy: I do, too.

Hal: Good.

The Hal and Cathy counseling session is worth rereading so that you won't miss any of the important dynamics of this brief dialogue:

1. Note Hal's almost exclusive use of Passive Listening, Acknowledgment Responses, and Active Listening.

2. Note how Cathy usually confirmed the accuracy of Hal's Active Listening responses with "Yeah," "It really is," "Right," "Yes, I am."

3. Note how Cathy progressed from the presenting problem (being behind in her work) to the more fundamental personal problem (needing to look good to others).

4. Note how Hal's Active Listening kept the ball with Cathy and how she took full responsibility for her own problem-solving and decision-making.

Most leaders naturally don't have the requisite listening skills to be counselors to their group members. Consequently, they miss countless opportunities to contribute to the personal development of the people they supervise, and to help subordinates meet their needs for self-esteem, achievement, and personal development. As I have repeatedly pointed out, meeting the basic needs of subordinates is an essential part of what makes leaders effective. But it takes listening skill as well.

THE LEADER AS A TEACHER

Leaders do a lot of teaching—giving instructions, explaining new policies or procedures, doing on-the-job training. Yet very few leaders have received special training to carry out this important function. They don't appreciate how difficult it is to teach people effectively—it is more complex than most people think.

In the first place, it is not commonly understood how much people resist being placed in the position of having to learn something new. It's hard work because it requires giving up accustomed ways of doing things and familiar ways of thinking about things. Learning requires change, and change can be disturbing—even threatening at times. Besides, the role of "a learner" in relation to "a teacher" is often felt as demeaning, no doubt because all of us remember being put down, punished, and patronized in school by our teachers. This means that, when leaders teach, they must avoid using teaching methods that will make their subordinates feel they're "being treated like children."

Take the all-too-typical situation of a leader who discovers that a group member is doing a task incorrectly and needs to be taught a better way. It may seem like just a simple and straightforward problem of correcting the subordinate's performance and teaching him the better way, but it seldom is that easy. Subordinates often respond with a variety of reactions: embarrassment, irritation, defensiveness, anger. Or, frequently, it may be difficult at first for the learner to understand the leader's instructions or to perform the task the new way. Usually, cues and clues reveal these reactions:

"I've always done it this way before."

"What's wrong with my way?"

"Nobody told me any different."

"Well, that might be *your* way of doing it."

"I don't get what you're telling me."

"Oh, I could never learn to do it that way."

"I feel so clumsy, it's not natural."

"You're going too fast."

"I don't get it—I must be dumb."

"I'll never learn how to do it that way."

These messages, it goes without saying, signal that the leader's intervention is causing the subordinate a problem. Remember your behavior rectangle:

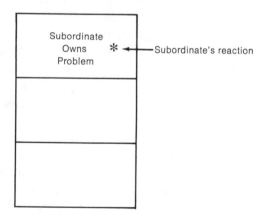

Having located the subordinate's reaction in the proper area of your rectangle, you know which skill is called for. Now is the time to demonstrate understanding, empathy, and acceptance by Active Listening. Little or no learning is going to occur until you acknowledge the subordinate's feelings and help him or her work through them somehow. Your teaching has to stop until you get evidence that the subordinate is again ready to learn.

This is the most important principle of effective teaching. Just as you can't be a leader without followers, you can't be a teacher without learners.

Another useful application of Active Listening helps in the teacher-learner relationship. We know that much more learning occurs when the learner is active in the process rather than passive. Yet a surprising amount of teaching casts the teacher as an active sender—that is, telling, explaining, lecturing, presenting—and the learner as a passive receiver. Getting learners more actively involved and participating in the learning process is the mark of an effective teacher.

One way of doing this is to give the learner more opportunity to talk about the subject, and, here again, Active Listening proves useful. The key is for you to give your presentations or instructions in very short segments, inviting your group members to give their reactions to these "mini-presentations." Then you employ Active Listening to demonstrate your understanding and acceptance of their messages.

This encourages learners to voice reactions to your teaching and promotes responses that will help you diagnose how much or how little of your instructions is actually being learned, so you can decide what further instruction is needed.

VI. HOW TO GET YOUR OWN NEEDS SATISFIED

Now that you have discovered how to be effective in helping others, you need to know how to help yourself. Why are some people so successful in getting their needs satisfied in their relationships with others? When someone's behavior is causing you a serious problem, how can you influence that person to change without making him or her lose face or feel resentment toward you?

Jane works too slowly and holds others up.

Your boss doesn't tell you things you need to know.

Howard invariably is late for meetings.

Mary is curt and impolite in handling phone calls with clients.

A supervisor of another department won't cooperate with you.

Laura doesn't answer letters promptly.

Frank volunteers to do jobs but often doesn't follow through.

One of your workers is much too slow.

Jan doesn't keep you informed about activities of her department.

Harry has an excessively high rate of turnover in his work group.

These, and countless others like them, are behaviors that belong in the bottom part of the behavioral rectangle, because they interfere with your getting your needs met.

Behaviors
Causing You
A Problem

You *own* these problems

Such problems require very different handling from that required when you are trying to help others with problems *they* own:

When Other Person Owns the Problem	When You Own the Problem
You're a listener	You're a sender
You're a counselor	You're an influencer
You want to help the other	You want to help yourself
You're a sounding board	You want to sound off
You facilitate the other's finding his or her own solution	You need to find a solution yourself
You can accept the other's solution; you don't need to be satisfied	You must be satisfied with the solution
You're primarily interested in the other's needs	You're primarily interested in your own needs
You're more passive	You're more assertive

When the other person owns the problem you employ *counseling skills.* When you own the problem you must employ *assertive skills.* And, assertive skills are distinctly different from counseling skills. Many leaders are nonassertive, so confronting people whose behavior causes them a problem is difficult for them, for a variety of reasons.

All of us are reluctant to tell other people that their behavior is unacceptable or is creating a problem for us. We run the risk that the other person will feel hurt, get angry, not like us. And such fears are not unwarranted. Who likes to hear that his or her behavior is unacceptable? People do frequently respond to confrontation with negative reactions that we don't like to hear. They may start an argument; they may retaliate with a critical message of their own; they may walk away hurt or angry; they may get defensive and disagreeable. So it takes a certain amount of courage to assert ourselves and confront others.

I have known unassertive leaders in organizations who just won't confront people. The price they pay, obviously, is that the problems rarely go away; they suffer in silent martyrdom or build up feelings of resentment toward the person causing the problem. It always feels unfair in relationships when the scales remain tipped against you and in favor of the other person. Tolerating an inequitable relationship is often labeled "permissiveness." And permissive leaders, like permissive parents, end up being the losers and not liking it.

Still another important reason why leaders approach the task of confronting with such trepidation is that the particular language they employ, originally learned from adults who confronted them as children, has a high probability of provoking resistance and retaliation or damaging the relationship with the person whom they confront. In our L.E.T. classes, instructors use a simple exercise, and its results consistently demonstrate that, when leaders confront people causing them a problem, the language of their confronting messages is abrasive, threatening, judgmental, moralizing, condescending, sarcastic, or injurious to the self-esteem of the person confronted. Take this situation:

Bill, one of your subordinates, repeatedly interrupts you and the other group members at your staff meetings, seriously reducing the effectiveness of the group's problem-solving. Today he did it again, so you decide to confront him after the meeting.

Here are some typical messages that leaders in our L.E.T. classes send in response to this simulated situation:

"For heavens' sake, Bill, let other people have their say before you make your points. Don't talk so much!" (ORDERING, DIRECTING).

"If you keep interrupting everyone in our meetings, Bill, you're going to have everyone mad at you" (WARNING, THREATENING).

"It is simple, common courtesy, Bill, to let people finish what they have to say before breaking in" (MORALIZING, PREACHING).

"God gave us two ears and one mouth so we would listen twice as much as we talk" (TEACHING, LECTURING).

"Bill, next time we have a staff meeting, may I suggest you hold back until everyone else makes their contribution" (ADVISING, OFFERING SOLUTIONS).

"Bill, you're really discourteous in our staff meetings" (CRITICIZING, JUDGING).

"Bill, I know you're very bright and you always have good ideas, but give others a break in our discussions" (PRAISING, BUTTERING UP).

"You act like Mr. Know-it-all in our staff meetings" (NAME-CALLING).

"I'm sure you can curb your habit of interrupting very easily, Bill" (REASSURING).

"I think you're using our meetings to show off your vast experience and knowledge" (PSYCHOANALYZING).

"Why do you have to hog the discussion so much and interrupt everyone?" (PROBING, QUESTIONING).

"Bill, you're going to have to do something about your shyness in our meetings—we never hear your opinions" (SARCASM, HUMOR).

While there are many variations on these themes, leaders typically confront others with messages that fall into one of these 12 categories. Do they sound familiar? They are the 12 Roadblocks again. And they are just as ineffective in confronting people when *you* own the problem as in counseling people when *they* own the problem.

Examine each of the 12 types and you will find they all contain a strong "You" component:

You stop it.

If *you* don't stop it, then . . .

You shouldn't do it.

You should know better.

You need to do this . . .

Why don't *you* try . . .

You are discourteous.

You are doing it because . . .

Why do *you* do it?

Here is what *you* ought to do.

It's obvious why I call such confrontations *You-mes-sages*. And people don't like to receive You-mes-sages. They carry a high risk of damaging relationships because

1. They make people feel guilty.

2. They may be felt as blame, put-downs, criticism, rejection.

3. They may communicate lack of respect for the other person.

4. They often cause reactive or retaliatory behavior.

5. They may be damaging to the recipient's self-esteem.

6. They can produce resistance, rather than openness, to change.

7. They may make a person feel hurt and, later, resentful.

8. They are often felt as punitive.

Apart from how they hurt your relationships, You-mes-sages usually fail to do what they are intended to accomplish—namely, influence the other person to change the behavior you find unacceptable. There are probably three reasons for this. First, people don't like to be told what to do (or not to do), so they dig in their heels and stubbornly resist any change. It's human nature for people to prefer initiating change themselves, when it becomes apparent their behavior is interfering with the needs of another. But You-messages usually deny people that opportunity, as for example: "Your letter contains a lot of careless typos. You'll have to do it over." Saying "You'll have to do it over" denies the typist the opportunity to *volunteer* to retype the letter, leaving no chance for earning some credit for offering to do so.

A second compelling reason for the ineffectiveness of You-messages is that they point the finger of blame at the recipient. They communicate, "You are at fault for causing me a problem," "You are bad," "You should have known better," "You are inconsiderate and thoughtless."

Blame is uncalled for in most situations. I suspect that

people are seldom aware their behavior is unacceptable to another. Their behavior is usually motivated only by a desire to meet their own needs, not by a deliberate intent to interfere with the needs of others. But when you send a You-message, you communicate, "You are bad for doing something to meet your needs"—a rather ridiculous notion, obviously.

Finally, You-messages are ineffective because they are "poor codes." Recall our diagram of the communication process and picture the sender coding and the receiver decoding. Remember that when someone's behavior is unacceptable to you, clearly you own the problem—you're the one who is worried, upset, burdened, disappointed, afraid, etc.

Take the example of a group member who forgets to return tools to the tool cabinet, which makes you upset because you waste a lot of your time looking in vain for the one you need. Obviously, the accurate code for your feelings would be

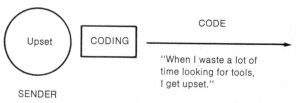

Note that this code contains "I's," not "You's." Whenever someone is causing you a problem, a clear and accurate code always would be in the form of an I-message: "I'm disappointed," "I hate to be interrupted," "I am worried," "I am frustrated," "I wasted a lot of time." A You-message refers to the other person and doesn't say anything about the feelings of the one owning the problem.

It is understandable why sending I-messages is sometimes called "leveling"—being open, honest, and direct with people in your life. Perhaps this is the source of the potency of I-messages. They communicate, "I am a human being who gets problems and feelings like every-one else." In a sense, an I-message is a *plea for help* from the person with a problem, and everyone knows how hard it is to ignore such an appeal. This is why I-messages are so likely to influence people to modify their behavior. Imagine yourself being on the receiving end of each of the following I-messages your supervisor might send, noting how you feel and whether it motivates you to modify your behavior out of consideration for your boss's needs:

1. "When I'm not kept informed about what's going on in your de-partment, I get worried and start imagining that you're having all kinds of problems that are not getting solved."

2. "When I hear about letters from potential clients not being an-swered for weeks at a time, I really get upset because I'm afraid we've lost some business and created a bad impression of our organization."

3. "When you're absent from our staff meetings, I feel strongly that our effectiveness is reduced because we don't have the benefit of your experience and knowledge in the marketing area."

4. "I really get anxious when I see that your costs are running consid-erably higher than budget, and I'm really puzzled when I don't see any corrective action being taken."

5. "When I saw the first drafts of our new product brochures, I was very disappointed in their quality; I'm afraid they're going to hurt our sales."

While undoubtedly you didn't feel joyously happy re-ceiving these messages (no one ever likes hearing that his or her behavior is unacceptable to another), you probably felt much more willing to modify your behavior than if you'd been told what to do, warned, put down, blamed, or lectured.

An L.E.T. graduate submitted the following account of confronting one of her supervisors in the Social Service Department of a city in Canada:

An extra office became available in the building in which I act as coordinator of services. I told George (a worker from another agency but providing programs and services from our building) to go ahead and use this office for storing some of his supplies and to feel free to fix up the room (paint, redecorate) so it would be suitable as a meeting place for some of his volunteers. However, I informed him that Susan, another worker, would still be using the office on Thursday evenings while supervising a Teen Drop-In Center. The Drop-In Center is adjacent to the shared office. The day George began fixing up the office I went back to see how things were coming along. The following is the conversation that took place.

Coordinator:	When you put up these no-smoking signs in the office and in the Teen Drop-In room, I wonder how the teenagers and Susan are going to accept it, and I become quite concerned.
George:	I think it's about time they learned that they don't need to smoke in this room—after all, the room isn't that large.
C:	You believe a rule needs to be laid down preventing smoking in this room.
G:	I sure do, and besides that, you told me to go ahead and fix up this office the way I want.
C:	You're wondering why I'm questioning you about the no-smoking signs when I gave you the go-ahead to fix up the office.
G:	Well, after all, you did seem to indicate that I could fix it the way I wanted.
C:	Yes, I did. However, I'm concerned about how the teens and Susan may react. There've been no complaints from them of a problem with smoking other than the fact that ashes may fall from a cigarette and burn a hole in the felt on the pool tables. What do you think we should so about this sign situation?
G:	Perhaps I could take the signs down from the Drop-In room and just leave one no-smoking sign up in the office.

C: You're willing to compromise.

G: Yes, in fact I think I won't put up any signs at all and just ask people not to smoke while I'm in the office.

C: You're willing to do without the signs completely then.

G: Yes, I am.

C: Do you feel OK about that?

G: Yes.

C: I think I will ask Susan to help us by enforcing a new rule within the Drop-In Center that there will be no smoking while standing around the pool table. This will prevent the tables being burned by ashes.

THE ESSENTIAL COMPONENTS OF AN I-MESSAGE

Have you ever had people confront you by telling you only how they felt—nothing more—such as,

"I'm upset with you."

"I'm really disappointed."

"I am worried."

"I am unhappy with you."

Such messages leave everyone puzzled and bewildered, so your first response was probably to ask *why* the confronter was upset, disappointed, worried, or unhappy. Or perhaps you responded with "What did I do?" The point is that telling a person only how you *feel* is an incomplete confrontation; it contains only one of the three components of a complete I-message: (1) a brief description of the *behavior* you find unacceptable, (2) your honest *feelings,* and (3) the tangible and concrete *effect* of the behavior on you (the consequences).

Obviously, to eliminate the necessity for the question, "What did I do?" you need to inform the person exactly what *behavior* you find unacceptable. Secondly, a direct and honest *expression of your feelings* is usually required in order to underscore the degree of emotional impact which the unacceptable behavior had on you. Lastly, you need to include the *effect* (or consequences) component in order to convince the person that you really have a logical, rational reason for wanting a behavior change (that your life is actually affected in some tangible and concrete way).

When people learn how to send I-messages, they find it extremely useful to remember this I-message formula: BEHAVIOR + FEELINGS + EFFECTS, not necessarily in that order.

During the initial phase of learning to send complete three-part I-messages you will feel self-conscious and mechanical. Gradually, with practice, they will come much more naturally and require less deliberate thought. But practice is required, as with almost any new skill: learning a new golf swing or tennis stroke, sailing a boat, learning to ski, or operating a calculator.

In the following example, taken from an interview with a plant manager, you will see a good three-part I-message and also get a feel for the changed attitudes of the supervisor towards his people:

"I have an old employee who thinks all the time he can remember numbers. His work is in the storeroom, and he feels he has it all stored up here in his memory. And his memory isn't that good, 'cause he consistently comes up with wrong numbers—more so than the new employees who don't trust their memory and look up and check and write down the right numbers. By bringing him in and setting him down I think I've got the problem across to him. And it has helped some. I told him, 'We've got a problem out there because you've gotten quite a few wrong tickets, and I'm really concerned about it because it really fouls up our bookkeeping on all this.' I gave him the *consequences* and the background.

And I said, 'As I grow older my memory isn't as good.' Now I didn't accuse him that his memory was flipping, and I think I brought it out in a roundabout way without putting him on the defensive. Well, he agreed that we had a problem and that it caused a lot of errors in our inventory. And it helped some, yes. I think he left with a better feeling, a better taste in his mouth than if I had given him the old 'Better straighten up and fly right or else' approach, you know. I think I don't underestimate the intelligence of people under me. That's one fallacy of management—they underplay or underrate people. I'll admit I had a little of that when I first became foreman, but now I realize that they actually are intelligent people. . . . I think anytime you can talk to someone in a way that doesn't downgrade him, you keep his respect. I feel he responds a hell of a lot better than when you say, 'I'm your boss and you do this or that.' If you can get to him in a way that he feels you're on a man-to-man basis and you've got a problem and you're only trying to solve it."

WHAT HAPPENS WHEN YOU SEND I-MESSAGES?

When you set out to influence someone to change by sending an I-message, a number of things can happen. Your initial message is only the first step in the change process, but it is important because it sets the tone for what may come later. For this discussion, I will sometimes use the terms "changer" and "changee."

Who Owns the Problem?

It is essential that you keep in mind the fundamental concept of "problem ownership." When you decide to try to change another person whose behavior is interfering with your getting your needs met, *you* own the problem, not the changee. The changee does not have a problem; indeed, he is getting *his* needs met by doing the very thing that causes you not to get *your* needs met. You can't blame a person for meeting his needs—it's the way people function. So don't be upset with *the person* whose behavior causes you a problem, although you are perfectly justified in being upset with *the fact* that you have a problem. This is the attitude that gets communicated by your nonblaming I-message, as opposed to a blaming You-message.

The Changee Is in the Driver's Seat

Although you assume responsibility for confronting the changee with the fact that you have a problem, in the final analysis it is the changee who ultimately must make the decision whether to change or not. The "locus of responsibility" resides in the changee. Because you have the problem, you are in fact *dependent on the changee.* Again, the I-message effectively and accurately communicates this attitude; it is a statement of your problem but does not tell the changee he must change or how he must change. Again I-messages are *appeals for help,* and this accounts for their often amazing potency. Most people respond better to honest appeals for help than to demands, threats, solutions, or lectures.

The Importance of "Shifting Gears"

Although I-messages are more likely to influence others to change than You-messages, still it is a fact that being confronted with the prospect of having to change is often disturbing to the changee. A common response of the changee to your I-message is to become anxious, upset, defensive, hurt, apologetic, or resistive, as in the following two examples:

1. Changer: I was really upset when I found several critical errors in your report because it made me look foolish at the board meeting where I presented the report.
   Changee: Well, you wanted it in such a hurry I didn't have time to double-check all my calculations.

2. Changer: When I hear complaints from patients that you are not answering their call light immediately, I get upset because I would hate to be held responsible for something bad happening to one of our patients.

   Changee: I can't be in two places at the same time, and besides some of our patients call us for things they can do themselves.

In both situations even your perfectly good I-message provoked defensiveness and some degree of hostility. Your I-message caused the changee a problem. Not at all unusual—people rarely like to be told their behavior is unacceptable, no matter how it is worded. When people resist changing, it is generally useless to keep hammering at them with subsequent I-messages; what is called for at such times is a quick shift to Active Listening. In these two situations the shift might sound something like:

1. Changer: You were under such a time bind, you felt you couldn't take the time to check your figures, is that right?

2. Changer: You mean you can't see the call light when you're in another patient's room. And I also gather you get irritated when patients call you to do things for them they could do themselves.

This shifting from a sending posture to a listening posture, which in our L.E.T. course is called "shifting gears," serves several extremely important functions in confrontation situations:

1. It communicates that the changer has understood and accepted (not agreed with, of course) the changee's position—his or her feelings, defenses, reasons. This greatly increases the changee's willingness to understand and accept the changer's position. ("He listened to me, now I'll listen to him.")

2. It helps dissipate the changee's emotional response (hurt, embarrassment, anger, regret), paving the way for possible change or, as I shall later describe, mutual problem-solving.

3. It results, not infrequently, in a change in the *changer*'s attitude —from previously finding the other's behavior unacceptable to later seeing it as acceptable. ("Oh, I now see why you miss some of the patients' call lights—you can't see them.")

After the changer has shifted gears to Active Listening, it might be appropriate to repeat the original I-message or send a modified one. ("I understand why you didn't recheck your calculations, but I still can't accept reports with incorrect figures.")

Here is an example of effective gear-shifting, reported by a supervisor who previously found it hard to confront people:

"I found it very difficult at first—actually using I-messages and then switching to Active Listening. Because I didn't like people to become very hostile with me. But it worked out very well one day at work. A girl came into my office when I was really busy working; I was under a lot of pressure. And this person likes to come in and sit and talk. If it hadn't been for L.E.T. and the Active Listening I probably never would have known how to handle the situation. So she came in, she sat down, and I delivered her an I-message: 'When you come into my office to sit down and talk, I can't get my work done and that really upsets me.' And so her automatic response was defensive and she in turn said, 'Well, what I wanted to talk about is also of concern to you.' And I kept above the emotion level and Active Listened her: 'Sounds like you're upset with me.' Yes, she was, she said. And I said, 'You feel hurt by my not wanting to listen to this issue right now.' And she said, 'Yes, I am hurt. I know you're busy, but surely you've got enough time for me.' And we came to the solution that we'd meet for lunch. So that worked out very well. . . . I guess I felt really good because this was the first time I had used an I-message in the work environment and been able to handle the defensiveness not as a direct slam on myself. It's a frightening thing to have to confront somebody with an issue. But once you start to realize that people normally will get defensive and that they can be talked into backing down by listening—I started to feel confident that I could deliver an I-message and then dwell on the other person's feeling, not my own."

Having learned in the L.E.T. class that people do frequently respond with defensiveness when confronted, this supervisor was able to overcome her fear of confrontation.

Augmenting a Person's Effort to Change

While a good I-message can often produce an immediate change in behavior, people sometimes need a good deal of support from a changer. Remember: people don't always have an easy time changing, because *behavior* change often requires giving up an entrenched, habitual way of doing things in favor of trying something novel and untested. This calls for the *changer* to participate more actively in the change process, usually only as a facilitator or catalyst, but sometimes in the more active role of a participant in joint problem-solving with the changee.

One effective way of augmenting a changee's change process is what I call "working the other person through the problem-solving process." Recall again the six steps of problem-solving:

I.   Identifying and defining the problem

II. Generating alternative solutions

III. Evaluating the alternate solutions

IV. Decision-making

V.   Implementing the decision

VI. Following up to evaluate the solution

Recall, too, that I defined an effective leader as "one who sees to it that problems get solved." This is exactly what the changers often must do after they confront a person;

they "stay with the changee" to help find and implement a solution that will be acceptable to the changee and the changer. Here is how this function was performed by one leader:

Supervisor:	Bob, I called you in because I have a problem. I'd thought after we had talked before about the quitting time, that you understood what our policy was, and that you intended to stick to it. So I was very surprised yesterday to see you leaving before five thirty. I'm kind of upset about it.
Worker:	Chuck, I've been trying awfully hard not to leave before five thirty. I hadn't left early in about two months until this emergency.
S:	You've had a good record recently. Sounds like yesterday was something special.
W:	I had a call in the middle of the afternoon from the guy I ride with who lives in my neighborhood. He said he had to leave right at five thirty and if I wasn't out on the street by then, he'd have to go on without me.
S:	Kind of put you in a bind, huh?
W:	Boy, I'll say! Once when he was sick I took the bus and it took me an hour and a half to get home.
S:	So you hated to use that alternative, huh.
W:	It only takes about a half hour riding with him.
S:	So you were torn between losing time and sticking to our rule.
W:	Yes, and I looked around for you in the afternoon. I guess you were out of the office because I couldn't find you.
S:	You hoped I'd approve if you could ask me.
W:	I was sure of it.
S:	Apparently you felt it was very important for you to go home and not miss your ride, even to the point of breaking a rule.

W: Well, it was a rare emergency that happens from time to time. Seems like a couple of minutes don't matter that much. I'm here working sometimes twenty minutes early in the morning.

S: I understand that. You're always here on time. But we have two policies—one policy of getting here on time and one of not leaving early—and both must be kept.

W: I wouldn't expect this to happen again, at least only very rarely.

S: I felt that after we had our last talk, Bob, but then something came up and it's happened again.

W: I told him then that I have to stay until five thirty, so he usually waits, except for yesterday. But he was nice enough to call.

S: Can you think of something you might do to avoid this thing in the future, because this rule is not to be broken unless there is an emergency more serious than this. I don't consider this to be the type of emergency that would warrant your leaving early. Can you think of anything that you could do to keep it from coming up again?

W: I could make sure that you know I'm leaving early, if he ever needs to leave again.

S: That solution doesn't satisfy me—I don't think I could agree. I don't think I could give my permission for this sort of emergency.

W: Not even ten or fifteen minutes?

S: Not for that. We should try to arrive at a solution that will satisfy you and satisfy me and the company policy.

W: Maybe I'd have to ride a bus on those days.

S: In other words, you can take a bus, if you have to.

W: I have. But it seems to me that the hour and a half it takes on the bus is a long time for just ten or fifteen minutes. Seems unreasonable, the policy that is.

S: Seems to you like, if you keep the policy most of the time, it's all right to break it once in a while.

W: It seems that way to me.

S: If the twenty people working in our department took the same attitude—almost every night someone would be leaving early. I wouldn't feel that would be fair.

W: No. Maybe I could find someone right here who could drive me home on those days. I wouldn't even mind walking a little way.

S: Think that would solve it, huh.

W: Yes. How would I go about finding someone?

S: I think Mr. Barrows has a list in the Personnel Department.

W: OK. I'll drop over there today.

S: Great. I appreciate your working this out, Bob.

Chuck, the supervisor, did a lot of Active Listening ("shifting gears") in this situation, but he also was a catalyst, helping Bob work through the six problem-solving steps: "Can you think of something you might do to avoid this thing in the future?" and "We should try to arrive at a solution that will satisfy you and satisfy me and the company policy." Chuck also helped Bob implement the decision he came to: "I think Mr. Barrows has a list in the Personnel Department."

On the other hand, Chuck always kept the locus of responsibility with Bob for deciding what to do. By Active Listening, he also communicated acceptance of the struggle Bob was having in changing. Yet Chuck did not back down from getting his own needs met—he was quietly but firmly assertive in communicating his own position to Bob.

Leaders often have to take an even more active role in helping subordinates change after confrontation. In one company where I worked as a consultant, the general manager became very unaccepting of his subordinates (division vice-presidents) when they did not hold staff meetings with their people. After he had confronted them, it became apparent that they lacked confidence in conducting participative staff meetings and letting decisions get made by the group. After listening to their anxieties, the general manager asked if they would allow him to attend one or two of each vice-president's staff meetings so he could observe and provide some training and coaching. They accepted that suggestion.

In addition to helping people change by training and coaching, leaders may need to provide group members with new data that give people feedback on how they are doing—e.g., monthly cost and revenue figures, sales records, production figures, and the like. For example, if you want your department heads to cut costs, you may need to provide them with periodic records of their actual costs.

How Much Do You Need to Know About the Changee?

My model for influencing people to change requires little or no "diagnostic" information about the changee. This is a different approach from the one traditionally used by most leaders in organizations. I call that the "diagnostic model" and mine the "confrontive model."

The diagnostic model requires leaders to get to know their people extremely well—their personality structure, their habitual ways of thinking and doing things, the reasons for their behavior. Such information, it is claimed, will help a leader know just what kinds of influence to bring to bear in order to get people to change.

The assumption implicit in the diagnostic model is that it is the leader who assumes responsibility for producing changes in group members, and the more leaders know *about* their people, the cleverer they will be in selecting methods for changing them. Too often this involves a subtle kind of manipulation; information about people is used to get them to buy the leader's *already determined* solutions. Perhaps you've heard, as I have, such statements as:

"What's the best approach to use with a person like Jim?"

"I don't know enough about what makes Karen tick to know what buttons to press."

"The way to get Hal to accept new procedures is to make him think they're his own ideas."

"You've got to treat women differently."

"I just can't figure out yet what Larry's problem is. He lacks motivation."

These statements come out of the "language of control," far more prevalent in the world of organizations and institutions than the "language of influence," from which the confrontive model is derived.

In the confrontive model the leader's understanding of Larry's problem is not nearly as important as Larry's own understanding of what his problem is.

In the confrontive model the leader doesn't need to think about what buttons to press to change Karen. It is far more important for the leader to confront Karen openly and honestly and help her find her own buttons.

In the confrontive model the leader couldn't care less about whether a person is a woman or man, old or young, liberal or conservative, an engineer or a salesman. The leader sees infinitely more similarities among humans than differences; besides, even if differences exist, the leader cares more about knowing *how* people feel than *why* they feel that way.

In the confrontive model what's behind people's feelings and behaviors is their business, not the leader's. The leader's business is to understand his or her own feelings and to communicate those feelings openly and honestly to others.

In the confrontive model leaders do not manipulate people on the basis of "personal case histories"; rather, they use methods of reaching solutions acceptable to both leader and group members.

Actually, the diagnostic model seriously handcuffs leaders, often deterring them from decisive action when subordinates cause them problems. For, when leaders feel it necessary to understand the whys and wherefores of subordinates' behavior before tackling a problem, they often never get around to it because they seldom get all the data they feel they need. People are complex, and it is next to impossible to acquire a complete understanding of "what makes them tick." Many leaders postpone or avoid action to solve human problems because of the paucity of their information about persons—information they feel they need to understand why certain people are unproductive, uncooperative, unenthusiastic, and so on.

With the confrontive model, leaders need only understand their own feelings and how to communicate them in a nonblameful way; then they need to put listening skills to work so they and their group members can work out mutually acceptable solutions.

Confronting and problem-solving with subordinates is simpler (and certainly more direct and straightforward) than trying to "figure people out" so you can better manipulate them toward a solution of your choosing.

VII. HOW TO MAKE YOUR MANAGEMENT TEAM EFFECTIVE

SOME leaders take the position that "a meeting is a group of people who individually can accomplish nothing but who collectively decide nothing can be done." Considering how unproductive and dull many group meetings are, it is not surprising that so many managers, administrators, and supervisors have such low regard for them and make such little use of them for problem-solving. Nevertheless, leaders rarely can do it on their own; and, as I pointed out in Chapter III, because they are not omniscient, leaders sorely need the resources of their group members to help them solve certain kinds of problems. So meetings are here to stay. I know of no other way to build an effective management team.

While they can't be avoided, most meetings certainly can be greatly improved—but not without considerable effort by the group leader.

Is it worth the effort for a leader to acquire competence in team building? In the long run, the benefits will be substantial, as I stressed in Chapter III: staff development, decreased dependence of members on their leader, greater identification with group goals, breaking down status differentials that act as barriers to honest communication, opportunity for members to meet their higher-level needs (affiliation, acceptance, self-esteem, and self-actualization), and in many cases higher-quality decisions derived from the wisdom of the group.

Such benefits, however, won't materialize unless leaders carefully consider such issues as who should attend management meetings, how to develop agendas, how to keep permanent records, the issue of confidentiality, rules for decision-making, and procedures for evaluating the group's effectiveness. In this chapter, I will discuss these important matters and will offer suggestions and guidelines to help leaders make their management team function much more effectively.

WHO SHOULD BE ON YOUR TEAM?

If you are going to build a team and use it to help you manage and solve problems, it is important for you to decide who is to be on the team and, equally important, for them to know, too.

Often the answer is determined simply by the organizational chart—all those for whom you are *directly* responsible, your total work group, as in this chart where you lead a group of five:

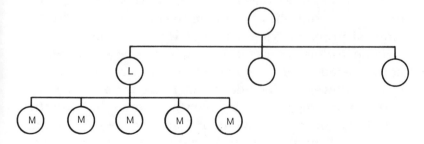

Some leaders, however, have been assigned additional people who perform certain "staff" functions, as opposed to "line" functions—secretaries, personnel directors, legal _advisors, staff assistants, as in this work group:

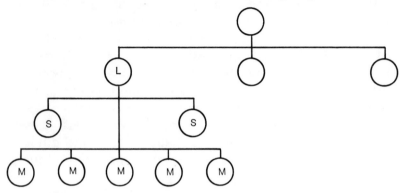

A leader with this type of group needs to decide whether or not to include his "staff" people on the management team. Do they have specialized knowledge not possessed by the "line" members? Do they want to attend regularly scheduled team meetings? Can you afford the time for them to attend? Are they people who need to be aware of all the group's problems (and their solutions) in order to function effectively? Are they persons who want to grow and become qualified to assume more responsible jobs in the organization? Is their knowledge so specialized that they would not have much to contribute, given the kinds of problems your group generally tackles?

Some leaders, after considering these questions, choose not to include "staff" people on their management team. Others do want to include them. There is no correct answer, yet my own bias is to give staff people the *opportunity* to be on the management team and see how things work out. Sometimes staff people decide for themselves they would prefer not to attend group meetings, for a variety of reasons: they feel they have little to contribute, they would rather do only their job, they dislike the give and take of problem-solving in groups, or they don't aspire to a position requiring further development. Obviously, such feelings must be respected and accepted.

Another alternative (I have tried it in my own organization) is to extend an open invitation for people in staff positions to attend management group meetings whenever the group is dealing with a problem in which they want to get involved. Such a policy neither excludes staff people nor requires them to attend when they don't want to.

Several years ago I tried unsuccessfully to enlarge my own management group meetings to include not only the six division heads reporting directly to me but anyone else in the organization who wanted to assume responsibility to participate in management problem-solving and decision-making. At that time there were only 25 employees in our organization, so I thought it might work. But a number of things influenced us to dispense with this procedure.

The size of the group made it very difficult to reach consensus; some people did not participate; some people dropped out; some people attended irregularly. I have since designated as my permanent management team only the eight people who report directly to me—both "line" and "staff." The nine of us meet once every two weeks. This group is responsible for all "management" decisions, yet anyone else may attend a particular meeting (or be invited) if the group is dealing with a problem about which they feel concern or have relevant data. As of this writing, I favor this arrangement and it seems to work well, but I don't discount the possibility that we might try yet another variation sometime in the future.

Organizations need to remain flexible to adapt to changes in personnel and to new objectives.

When the members of your management team have been identified, you may also want to consider having each member designate an alternate, who attends your management meetings in the absence of the permanent member. This policy makes it unnecessary for the group to delay making a decision that would affect the department whose representative is absent; and it provides training and development for the alternate.

What if a leader has so many members in his or her group that problem-solving and decision-making is too difficult or time-consuming? (In many schools, the principal may be responsible for as many as 50 teachers. A management group of this size is usually very unwieldy.)

One feasible option is a form of "representative" government. All the teachers would elect a much smaller number to serve on the principal's management team—perhaps one teacher for each grade level or one for each subject-matter specialty. Elections could be held each year or every other year, so over a period of time all teachers could serve on the management team.

DIFFERENT KINDS OF MEETINGS

One reason why group meetings are ineffectively used, or not used at all, is that leaders lack a coherent "theory" about meetings and the various functions they are meant to serve. They employ one kind of meeting when they should have employed another. Or they use one meeting to accomplish several objectives, instead of using several meetings, each accomplishing only one objective. Without guidelines, leaders find their meetings turn into kaffeeklatsches, endless discussions with nothing accomplished.

First, think of meetings as falling into two categories:

1. Informational
2. Problem-solving.

Informational meetings are for such purposes as personal growth, continuing education, keeping informed about what other group members are doing (including the leader). In such meetings no problem-solving should be attempted, and usually it is unnecessary to limit the number of participants. Informational meetings would be appropriate for such functions as

1. The leader (or a group member) gives a report to the group on what he or she learned at a conference or a site visit to another organization.

2. An outside consultant is employed to tell the group about something innovative or promising.

3. Each group member (say they are department heads) informs all the others what is going on in his or her department.

4. The leader routinely reports to his or her group what actions were taken or decisions made in the management group one level above in which the leader is a group member.

In such informational meetings, questions can be asked or comments permitted, but it is important that no problem-solving (and of course no decision-making) occur. Should problems arise—and often they do—they should be placed on the agenda for the next Problem-Solving Meeting.

There are several different kinds of Problem-Solving Meetings, each associated with one or more of the six steps of the problem-solving process with which you are already familiar:

The Problem Identification Meeting (Step I).

The Solution Generating Meeting (Step II).

The Evaluation and Decision-Making Meeting (Steps III and IV).

The Implementation Meeting (Step V).

The Regularly Scheduled Management Meeting (Steps I through VI).

The Problem Identification Meeting

All organizations have problems, and these should not be considered "bad" or pathological. An organization without many problems is one that is not growing, changing, adapting.

Unfortunately, organizational leaders do not always know what problems exist. They are removed from operational levels where problems emerge. And subordinates are often reluctant to admit the existence of problems to their superior. They feel it is too risky—they'll be adversely evaluated or censured. Finally, problems often remain unsolved in the daily routine of getting things done.

Leaders must make a deliberate effort to discover and identify problems. They must "go to the problems" because the problems may not always come to them.

The Problem Identification Meeting is one method for doing this. Such a meeting may involve all of a leader's subordinates or only some. The meeting may be called once a month or once every several months.

The objective of the Problem Identification Meeting is very limited: to identify as many problems as possible in a specified time period without considering any solutions.

The leader may choose to stay out of the meeting to remove any fears the group members may have about being judged by the leader. If a nonevaluative climate exists in the group and members are accustomed to revealing problems without judgment or censure, the leader may choose to participate in the meeting, confident that his presence will not inhibit problem identification.

Simple techniques can facilitate the process. There is the "slip method": participants anonymously write each problem on a slip or a card and place them in a box. In the "chalkboard method" the leader (or any group member) writes each problem on a chalkboard or chart pad for everyone to see. The identification of the person submitting each problem may be indicated by writing the initials of the person after the problem, or identification may be eliminated altogether.

The leader's role is not at all complex. He or she first must "structure" the meeting: define the purpose, explain the procedure, spell out the ground rules (no evaluation, no raising of hands for permission to speak, no documentation, no long-winded examples or illustrations, no solutions), set the time limit. If problems are submitted orally, the leader may use Active Listening to clarify each group member's message and to demonstrate his or her acceptance (nonevaluation) of the person generating the problem.

One special application of the Problem Identification Meeting is when important changes are forthcoming that will affect your group: new policies coming down from higher levels, the impending introduction of new methods, new equipment, new forms, etc. The question posed to the group would be something like:

"What possible problems do you see arising in our group as a result of the forthcoming change in ———?"

Used in this connection, the Problem Identification Meeting is an excellent vehicle for leaders to perform one of the requirements for effective leadership in formal organizations: helping group members deal constructively with the impact of changes on their lives. The response to change depends on how the change is *interpreted* by those on whom it impacts. Their particular interpretation will reflect how well they are psychologically prepared for the change and how well they feel they can cope with it. Obviously, full participation in identifying problems they feel might arise from a change is an important beginning toward helping people cope with it, as illustrated in the following excerpt from an interview with a manager:

"Using Method III [see Chapter VIII] is out of character for some of the foremen. They're used to operating a certain way and they feel like they'd be phony if they changed. Some of them do use Method III now. They get their people participating more in some of the problems and decisions. Like buying a new piece of equipment. There were the scooters, also the new iron worker and the drill press. It does make a difference because before, when we bought something new in the shop, the mechanics would find four hundred and fifty things wrong with it. Now they have a part in picking it out and a voice in where to put it. We haven't had any bitching on the iron worker, the drill press, and the new scooters, they think, are terrific."

Some leaders periodically get their group together only to air gripes and grievances and uncover problems. One supervisor we interviewed told how he made effective use of the Problem-Identification Meeting.

"When we have an open discussion meeting now, I tell them, 'If there's anything anybody wants to talk about, I don't care what it is, just bring it out in the open. I'll listen to you or give my opinions about it.' And if it's something pertaining to something I'm doing I'll always ask, 'What do you think of me as a boss?' And I get some hell of a lot of good answers. I just lay it on the line and say, 'Hey, it's just you and I—I'm not management and you're not hourly wage people. We're two individuals. I want to know what you think about me and I'll tell you what I think about you.' And I find that it works real well in most cases. . . . They have problems and I have problems. And we sit down and discuss it. I'm trying to get my message over and I'm trying to listen to what they're telling me. I'm not the smartest guy in the world—you had guys in the L.E.T. course that grasped things quicker than I did. But I always figure if I get just one thing out of a course, I've accomplished a lot. It has made me have a better tendency to look at the people that are working for me."

The Solution-Generating Meeting

This type of meeting is often called a "Brainstorming Meeting," a term probably first coined by Alex Osborne to describe a method to help bring out the creativity of groups faced with a problem to solve. The group takes a problem (could be one identified in a Problem Identification Meeting) and focuses its energies only on alternative solutions:

How can we cut down on the frequency and duration of long-distance phone calls?

How can we reduce paper work?

What can we do to increase sales of such and such product?

What could we do in our school to make learning more exciting for kids?

What could we do to approach zero defects in the manufacturing of such and such product?

How can we improve patient care in the hospital?

Because creativity does not flourish in a climate of judgment and evaluation (nonacceptance), formal brainstorming sessions should be governed by certain ground rules:

No evaluation of any kind.

Anything goes, "freewheel," let your mind go, don't censor your own ideas.

Piggyback on ideas from others.

Look at the problem from many different frames of reference.

Because quantity is what is wanted, group members are cautioned against trying to justify or document their ideas —make them brief and keep up a fast pace.

Someone in the group (often the leader but not necessarily) writes the ideas down quickly on cards, a chalkboard, or chart pad. Later they can be classified or categorized to make it easier for the next step—evaluation (usually done at a later meeting).

The leader's principal functions are to listen for evaluations and remind the group that they are prohibited, to encourage the group to think creatively, and to keep up a fast pace. When time is up, groups like to hear all their ideas read off, unless of course they were written on the board or chart pad.

These meetings can be fun; they usually generate enthusiasm and excitement. Universally, group members express amazement at the quantity and uniqueness of their solutions.

The Evaluation and Decision-Making Meeting

When problem identification and/or solution-generating have been accomplished in previous meetings, leaders may convene a special meeting to continue the problem-solving process through Steps III and IV—Evaluation and Decision-Making. Ordinarily these two steps are best combined, since evaluation leads naturally into making a decision on which of the solutions is (or are) best.

Unlike the first two types of meetings, the Evaluation and Decision-Making Meeting usually runs more effectively with a limited number of participants. Beyond 12 to 15 participants it becomes quite ineffective in making decisions by consensus, and then groups make the mistake of falling back on a voting procedure to arrive at decisions. (More about the disadvantages of voting later.)

The Implementation Meeting

A leader may convene a separate meeting solely for the purpose of enlisting the participation of group members in determining how a previously made decision is to be implemented—*who* does *what* by *when*? I have watched many management groups arrive at high-quality decisions only to neglect the equally important step of working out plans for implementing those decisions.

While it is certainly possible for leaders to carry out this task alone, arbitrarily assigning responsibility to different members of the group for implementing the various parts of a decision, it should not be overlooked that group members possess a lot of relevant information that can influence how a decision is best put into action: who has prior and appropriate experience, who has available time, who *wants* to be involved in implementation and who does not, who has sufficient staff help, who has the relevant resources (knowledge, data, skills, equipment), and so on. Utilizing the participation of group members frequently produces better plans for making decisions work than when the leader assumes this responsibility him or herself.

The Regularly Scheduled Management Meeting

I am often asked what I consider the most important requirement for leadership effectiveness. My answer always is, "Regularly scheduled problem-solving and decision-making meetings with your management team." Implied is that leaders learn how to conduct the meetings effectively.

To adapt an old cliché: "Show me an ineffective organization or group and I'll give you a leader who either does not have management meetings at all or who conducts them poorly." While that may strike some as an overgeneralization, my years of experience as a consultant to many kinds of organizations and groups have given me confidence in the validity of that assertion.

At the risk of sounding academic, I should add that most textbooks and journal articles in the field of organizational management show rather consistent agreement among experts that the effectiveness of leaders is highly correlated with their commitment to (and advocacy of) such concepts as "team building," "participative management," "two-way communication," "mutual need satisfaction," "group cohesiveness," "equitable social exchange relationships," "Theory Y" (Douglas McGregor's heavily collaborative and participative theory of leadership), and the approach called "Model II" by Argyris and Schon (a democratic approach involving leaders' sharing power with anyone having competence, plus maximizing the contributions of each group member).

These ideas will remain empty abstractions for the intellectual entertainment of professors and students in university business schools unless leaders in our society can be influenced to institute management meetings and be taught how to make them work.

In Chapter III, I listed a number of arguments for participative management meetings. Now I offer guidelines for making them operate effectively.

GUIDELINES FOR MAKING MANAGEMENT MEETINGS WORK

Many administrators, managers, or supervisors have little conception of what it takes to set up regularly scheduled management meetings and make them function effectively. Smooth and efficient problem-solving groups don't just happen; they develop over time. Based on my experience in helping leaders develop effective management groups, I have identified 17 separate procedural or structural problems that leaders and their groups must deal with.

Not all my guidelines will be appropriate for every group. Some are more appropriate for meetings at middle and upper management levels than at the level of first-line supervision. Also, some suggestions are for what a leader should *ideally* do; in practice, conditions might prevent leaders following certain of my guidelines—as, for example, meeting in a conference room with chalkboards and chart pads. (I have seen effective team meetings where the members sat in the corner of a factory on old wooden stools.)

Finally, I should emphasize that these guidelines are for leaders who are ready, in philosophy and attitude, to develop their group members into a cohesive problem-solving and decision-making team, with opportunity for all members to participate in *each of the six steps of the problem-solving process.*

1. Frequency of Meetings

How often a group needs to meet is an individual matter depending on the number of problems the group has to solve, the complexity of the problems, and the effectiveness of the group.

Preferably, groups should meet at the same time, on the same day, on a regularly scheduled basis.

Newly formed groups often have to meet more frequently at first because of their inexperience and full agenda.

A group will build up experience that will tell how frequently it needs to meet in order to get its problems solved.

It may be appropriate for some groups to meet for a

short period in the morning, every day. Groups should meet and carry on as usual even in the absence of one of the members or *even in the absence of the leader.*

2. Duration of Meetings

Meetings should begin and end at specific and rigidly enforced times.

Groups should not meet longer than two hours without a break.

It is better to set up additional meetings than have a single meeting that is too long.

After some experience, the group should be allowed to decide the length of its meeting, taking into consideration organizational needs and the fatigue factor.

3. Priority of Meetings

The group should decide at the outset on the importance of its meetings compared with other organizational requirements.

Preferably, very few other organizational requirements should have greater priority than attendance at the group meetings.

Each group member should assume full responsibility for having his or her phone calls held so he or she is not called out of the meeting.

The group may wish to delegate responsibility to the leader for making decisions about when some other requirement is more important than a person's attendance at the group meeting.

4. Alternates for Members

It should be the responsibility of each group member to appoint an alternate to attend group meetings in the member's absence.

Each group member should assume responsibility for keeping his or her alternate informed at all times so the alternate has sufficient knowledge to be a responsible member.

Each group member should delegate to alternates full authority to speak for their departments when in the group meeting.

5. Place of Meeting

Meetings held in conjunction with lunches or dinners out of the plant are seldom effective.

Conference rooms with adequate seating facilities, privacy, quiet, and comfort are preferred sites.

6. Physical Arrangements

Blackboards or chart pads should be available at all meetings.

Members should be seated so that each person can be seen by every other person.

The leader should minimize status by not always sitting at the head of the table. Preferably, tables should be provided to enable group members to write notes.

Coffee should be available and members free to get coffee when they want it.

7. The Recording Function

The group should set up its own appropriate methods for recording the group proceedings.

Some groups have a permanent recorder; others rotate the recording function. It is inadvisable for the leader to be the recorder; his or her time should be free for other functions.

The group should decide what it wants recorded. Preferably, the group should record only decisions, the plans for dealing with unresolved problems, problems emerging from discussion that are to go on future agendas, task assignments, and follow-up action.

After recording some specific action of the group, recorders should test out their understanding of that action on the total group to make sure that they have recorded it accurately.

Notes should not be made of the discussions leading up to group decisions. The briefer the record of the group proceedings, the more likely it is to be read and reviewed later.

A very useful format for recording decisions is (1) a brief statement of the problem, and (2) *who* does *what* by *when.*

8. Developing the Agenda

The group, rather than the leader, should own its own agenda. This is critical.

Groups can have formal agendas prepared ahead of time by members assuming responsibility for submitting agenda items to someone who makes a list, which is then sent out to all members prior to the meeting. Or members can write items on a conveniently located chart pad during the week.

Groups may prefer to develop the agenda at the start of each meeting, in which case members are asked at the beginning of each meeting for items for the agenda. These are written on the blackboard or chart pad. Don't discuss any agenda item until the list is completed.

Agendas prepared ahead of time have the advantage of informing group members which problems are going to be tackled, so they may make adequate preparation. Even where there is an agenda prepared ahead of time, the group should have a procedure for soliciting additional agenda items at the beginning of the meeting, in case new problems emerged after the formal agenda was prepared.

9. Establishing Priorities for Agenda Items

The group should establish some procedure for determining the relative importance of each agenda item, so that the most important items can be taken up first. This can be done quickly at the start of each meeting, or, in the case of the prepared agenda, those who submit items should indicate how crucial each item is. The group then can set priorities at the start of each meeting.

Each group member must assume responsibility for informing the group of the degree of importance of his or her agenda items, in contrast to the usual practice of deferring to the leader's agenda items.

10. Rules for Speaking

The group should work out its own rules for handling communication during the meeting.

Preferably, there should be a minimum of rules, or none at all. Effective problem-solving groups usually function quite informally, permitting group members to speak when they feel like it without getting permission from the leader.

In mature problem-solving groups, each member assumes sole responsibility for the appropriateness and timing of his or her own contributions as well as for facilitating communication from others.

The leader must be especially careful not to inhibit others' contributions by dominating or controlling the group's communication. He or she has to overcome the tendency for people to feel inhibited in the presence of the person in the leadership position.

11. Kinds of Problems Appropriate for the Group

Every member of the group should have a clear notion of the kinds of problems that are appropriate for the group.

Generally, problems appropriate for the group are (1) those most likely to require data from group members for their solution, and (2) problems whose solutions may affect the members of the group or may have to be implemented by the members of the group.

Group members assume responsibility for determining the appropriateness of problems they bring to the group and for screening out problems that affect only their own area of responsibility.

Groups should always be alert to items that are not appropriate to the total group and quickly assign them to some individual or individuals who will resolve them outside of the group meeting.

Each person, including the leader, should tell the group exactly what his or her agenda item requires from the group: (1) a decision, or (2) their ideas for solution, after which he or she will pick the final solution, or (3) a sounding board to test out the solution he or she has tentatively chosen.

12. Kinds of Problems Inappropriate for Meetings

The group should never use its time for solving problems (1) that concern only a few of its members, (2) that are too unimportant for the level of the group, (3) that require staff study and preliminary data gathering, or (4) that are outside the area of authority of the group.

All members should assume responsibility at all times for expressing themselves when they feel a particular problem is inappropriate for the total group.

13. Rules for Decision-Making

Preferably, groups should strive for total agreement on all problems. If there is sufficient time, the group should keep discussing a problem until it reaches a solution agreeable to everyone.

When group members do not feel particularly strong about the correctness of their position, they should be willing to go along with the majority.

Group members should be particularly sensitive to times when further advocacy of their position is unlikely to change the position of the majority.

Never vote unless it is a straw vote to determine how the group is lining up on a particular problem.

For some kinds of problems, the group members should be willing to defer to those members who will have more responsibility for implementing a particular solution, or to those members into whose area the problem most logically falls.

When time does not permit enough discussion to obtain total agreement, the group may delegate the final decision to one member, two or three members acting as a subgroup, or to the leader.

14. Confidentiality of Group Meetings

It is extremely important that each group member assume responsibility for keeping confidences. In effective problem-solving groups members feel that they may express any feeling or opinion and be assured that the other members will not quote them or report their comments to people outside the group.

The only thing that members should assume is safe to discuss outside the group is what has been recorded in the minutes.

In some cases, the group may decide that a particular decision should not be discussed outside the group, or the group may set certain conditions governing discussion of a particular matter outside the group.

The attitude of each group member should be that he or she is a member of a family and that what goes on in the family discussion should not be communicated to people outside the family.

15. Disposition of Agenda Items

At each group meeting, every agenda item should be disposed of in one of several ways: (1) a solution reached, (2) the problem delegated for further study outside the group, (3) the problem delegated to an individual or subgroup for a recommendation to the total group, (4) the problem placed on the agenda of a future meeting, (5) the problem taken off the agenda by the member who submitted it, or (6) the problem redefined in other terms.

In no case should a problem be left hanging.

16. Minutes of the Meeting

Minutes should be typed and distributed to all members of the group as soon as possible after the meeting.

The group should set up definite rules on who should be permitted to see the minutes and who, in addition to the group members, should receive copies.

Individual members of the group should personally communicate important outcomes of the meeting to subordinates, rather than run the risk of subordinates misunderstanding the minutes.

If a secretary types and duplicates the minutes of the meetings, that person should be instructed about the confidentiality of the minutes.

Minutes of each meeting should contain at least the following: (1) all decisions reached by the group, (2) a record of the disposition of every agenda item, (3) all task assignments, including due dates: WHO does WHAT by WHEN.

17. *Procedures for Continual Evaluation of Group Effectiveness*

Let's face it: groups, like individuals, do not always function effectively. Learning is facilitated by immediate feedback of results. Thus, effective groups usually build in specific procedures for evaluating their own effectiveness.

The group should adopt or devise some method for evaluating its own functioning. Some groups do this at the end of each meeting; others do it periodically but less frequently. Some use written evaluation sheets; others evaluate orally.

RESPONSIBILITIES OF THE MEMBERS IN MANAGEMENT MEETINGS

A management team will never function effectively in its meetings unless all members learn to carry out certain important functions and assume certain responsibilities. While everyone accepts that effective leadership behavior is critical for the success of meetings, seldom do we hear anything about *effective membership behavior*. Yet how members behave can make or break management meetings. It is no exaggeration, on the basis of my experience, that most group members do not know the first thing about how to function effectively in a participative problem-solving group. How could they? In all their lives most people have never been in such a group. This means that when you decide to start management meetings you'll be handicapped by having very inexperienced group members. The cards are stacked against you even more, for most of your group members will have had plenty of experience participating in autocratically run meetings where leaders allowed members no chance to participate constructively.

You will recall the earlier discussion of how leaders

"inherit the coping mechanisms" of their people—patterns of behavior they learned in previous relationships with authoritarian leaders. For you to build a team that works effectively in your management group meetings, you are faced with the task of replacing these coping mechanisms with more constructive behaviors.

Just being a different kind of leader from those your people have known will bring about *some* changes in the behavior of your group; they will begin to model your behavior. But you can do more: providing your group members with some instruction, teaching them guidelines for desirable "membership behavior." This will be an eye-opener to your people because so much of it will be new to them. Your instruction will also help them understand clearly your expectations for their behavior in your group meetings.

Responsibilities of Group Members Before Each Meeting

1. Reread the minutes of the previous meeting as a check on whether you have completed all task assignments for the previous meeting.

2. Make necessary arrangements to avoid being called out of the meeting by phone calls or visitors.

3. Plan so you can get to the meeting on time.

4. Have clearly in your mind the items you want to put on the agenda.

5. Be prepared with any materials or data you need to furnish the group to help them deal with your agenda items.

6. If the agenda is available ahead of time, study it to see whether you need preparation to discuss the problems intelligently.

7. If you must be absent, inform and prepare your alternate.

Responsibilities of Group Members During Meeting

1. Be sure to submit your items for the agenda. State them very clearly—do not elaborate.

2. When you have an opinion or feeling, state it honestly and clearly—don't sit on feelings.

3. Stay on the agenda item being dealt with and help others stay on it.

4. When you don't understand what someone is saying, ask for clarification.

5. Participate actively—when you have something to say, say it.

6. Assume responsibility for making process contributions—inputs that will facilitate the problem-solving process, such as

Asking questions

Keeping the group on the track

Calling for the decision

Clarifying members' statements

Summarizing

Listening to others

Getting the agenda set quickly

Getting things on the board or chart pad

7. Protect the rights of others to have their opinions or feelings heard—encourage silent members.

8. Listen attentively to others—clarify what others are saying when appropriate.

9. Try to think creatively about solutions that might resolve conflicts—try them out on the group.

10. Avoid communications that disrupt a group—humor, sarcasm, diversions, asides, jokes, digs.

11. Keep notes on things you agree to do after the meeting.

12. At all times, keep saying to yourself, "What, right now, would help this group move ahead and get this problem solved? What can I do to help this group function more effectively? What does the group need? How can I help?"

Responsibilities of Group Members After Meeting

1. Carry out assignments and commitments.

2. Pass on to your subordinates decisions or information that they should know about.

3. Keep confidential anything said or done in the meeting except for final decisions.

4. Refrain from complaining about a decision that you agreed to. Don't pass the buck.

5. Refrain from "out-of-meeting appeals" to the leader. Your feelings about the group should be expressed in the group.

6. Don't appeal to the leader to reverse a decision. Bring it up at the next meeting.

THE SPECIAL RESPONSIBILITIES OF THE GROUP LEADER

Obviously, if we think of the leader of the management team as also being a member, everything in the previous section applies as much to the leader as to the members. However, leaders usually have special responsibilities in management meetings by virtue of their unique position in the group as well as being seen by the group members as having roles different from them. After all, in formal organizations leaders do possess more "authority," and they always have the ultimate accountability for the success or failure of the group. The special status of the leader's position makes it necessary for him or her to carry out certain special functions.

It is one thing for leaders to *tell* their group that they want to build a problem-solving and decision-making management team, but their words must be reinforced by what they do. In one organization in which I served as a consultant to the top management group, one of the members, a vice-president, had this to say about their management meetings:

"We've been told by Dave [the company president] that he wants us to be a democratic group and make group decisions, but he always has the decision in his back pocket. We're supposed to discuss problems and come up with decisions, but they have to be *his* decisions. I just go along for the ride and keep my mouth shut. Why waste time participating when we know it's always going to end up with the boss getting his way?"

My own observations of their management meetings confirmed what the vice-president felt—the president was not practicing what he preached. And he was not fooling any of his group members. They knew he was unwilling to trust the wisdom of the group and allow the decision-making responsibility to be taken over by the total group.

I have observed other leaders who espoused the idea of fostering a "safe climate" in which group members felt free to state their opinions and disagree with the leader's, yet in the management meetings these leaders were unable to curb their tendencies to use such Roadblocks as negative evaluation, moralizing and preaching, lecturing, and psychoanalyzing. As a result, their group members were afraid to be open and honest in meetings; the risks of being put down were too great.

During the early stages of trying to get a group to become responsible, leaders often must bend over backwards to avoid inhibiting participation by members, as well as behavior that will be seen as controlling or running the group. This may mean that early in the game you should limit your own contributions to those verbal responses that foster a climate of acceptance and nonevaluation. Your principal communication tools for creating such a climate are Active Listening, Passive Listening, Door Openers, and Acknowledgment Responses. Taking a more active role before the members have decreased their dependence on you or lost their fear of your evaluation is risky. As a leader, you cannot become a more fully functioning participant until your group members gain enough security to participate freely and to accept or reject your substantial contributions on their merit, as they do those of other group members.

In time, once group members begin to believe you mean it when you say it is not *your* group, but *ours,* once they begin to sense that it is safe for them to make contributions, and once they feel certain that you are not subtly manipulating them toward your preconceived solutions—then you will be viewed more as another member than as *the* leader. When this happens it will be safer for you to participate more actively and more fully. But it takes time.

How do leaders know exactly when group members reach the stage of seeing them more as members than as leaders? You never know *exactly* when, yet there are certain cues indicating the readiness of a group for you to act like any other group member:

Group members address you no more formally than they do others in the group.

Group members won't look to you to start the meeting (or end it).

Group members address their remarks to each other rather than to you alone.

Group members speak up spontaneously without asking your permission.

Group members start to disagree with you or question your opinions.

Bright ideas originate from many members of the group.

The group arrives at decisions without checking with you as the final judge.

Group members utilize the resources and experiences of others rather than depend on yours alone.

Group members play an active role in making "process contributions" —those that improve the group's functioning.

Group members themselves confront other members who are disrupting the group or hindering progress rather than look to you to confront them.

From my experiences with groups—in my own organization and consulting with other organizations—certain principles or guidelines have emerged which seem to have relevance for leaders as they start to build their group into an effective management team:

1. The more dependent the group is on its leader, the more his or her contribution will inhibit the participation of other members.

2. The greater the status or prestige differential between the leader and the members (as perceived by the members), the more likely the leader's contributions will inhibit participation of the members.

3. Once a leader becomes like "another member" of the group, any tendency for him or her to participate too frequently can be dealt with by the group much more easily than when he or she is perceived as *the* leader. People feel free to exert some control over the participation of *members,* whereas they are more afraid to try curbing the participation of the *leader.*

4. A leader's awareness of the potentially inhibiting effect of his participation on that of the members helps control his or her participation. This awareness probably makes the leader more sensitive to seeing certain subtle signs that indicate that group members are inhibited.

5. Finding the appropriate balance between listening to others and contributing one's own ideas in group discussion is a problem not

only for the leader but also for each member. Even when a leader successfully reduces his leadership role and thus acquires membership, he still is faced with the problem of finding a balance between listening and sending.

6. Once seen by group members as another member of the group, a leader's contributions are more likely to be accepted or rejected on their merits, as opposed to being either accepted uncritically by the group or resisted (because of the members' reaction to the leader as an authority figure). This is to say that in the early stages of a group's development, the formal leader's contributions will have a far different effect on the group than they will in later stages when the group begins to react to the leader more as another member rather than as the formal leader.

VIII. CONFLICTS: WHO SHALL WIN, WHO SHALL LOSE?

A conflict, according to one unabridged dictionary, is a collision or disagreement, a controversy or quarrel, a clash or collision, a battle or struggle—especially a prolonged struggle. The word connotes something serious and intense. And, as everyone knows from experience, conflicts are unpleasant and disruptive in relationships, as well as counterproductive and costly for a group or organization. Yet it is difficult to escape the conclusion that some conflicts are *inevitable* in human relationships. So that leaves two tasks: discovering how to minimize conflicts and how to resolve those that cannot be prevented.

While conflicts can never be completely avoided in relationships between people, certainly some can be prevented, particularly if leaders use the skills and methods described in previous chapters. These and other related skills help prevent situations from escalating into full-blown power struggles.

The Listening Skill. A leader who becomes competent in helping group members or associates solve problems *they* own will be doing a job of prevention. After all, problems of subordinates might affect their performance on the job, which obviously could then cause the leader a problem and possibly create a conflict between them.

Suppose one day you get cues or clues that one of your group members seems unusually morose and preoccupied. While this behavior is not in any way unacceptable to you—everyone gets that way sometimes—nevertheless you are worried that, if it continues for several days, his job performance might suffer because at this time you are dependent on this person completing an important project. Certainly it would be prudent to make the effort to approach him and ask if you could help: "Bob, I noticed today you seem to have something on your mind that's bothering you. Would it help to talk about it? I've got some time now."

Often, a few minutes of listening to a person can do wonders: his feelings come out in the open and get dissipated, problem-solving gets started, and he may even arrive at some solution. An added dividend is that you have demonstrated that you care about the person. And if the problem gets solved, your listening has served the function of *prevention*. You have prevented the occurrence of subsequent behavior that would indeed be unacceptable to you—as, for example, his failure to complete the project.

The Confrontive Skill. Obviously, the purpose of directly confronting someone is to influence him or her to change some behavior that is causing you a problem. A good I-Message increases your chance of accomplishing that; the effects will be the prevention of some conflict later developing between you and that person, as in this situation:

Manager: I have to tell you what's on my mind, Sam. When I travel around the state and hear some of our best customers complain about late deliveries, I first get embarrassed and then upset, because I'm afraid we're going to lose some of those accounts.

Sam:	Yeah, I don't blame you, Lloyd. I guess you don't know I've been shorthanded out here for two weeks.
Manager:	No, I didn't know. I wish I had known before now. I feel very strongly that we should never let being shorthanded hurt our customer relationships.
Sam:	How can we prevent that, Lloyd? Hire temporary help?
Manager:	That's certainly one thing you could do.
Sam:	I didn't think I had the authority to do that. That ups the costs, you know.
Manager:	You didn't feel free to make that decision on your own.
Sam:	That's right.
Manager:	Could we have an understanding, Sam, that in the future you do have the authority to hire a temporary person, but if you ever need more than one, you get together with me?
Sam:	OK by me. I like that. I think that'll solve the problem.
Manager:	I do, too, Sam. It'll relieve me of a lot of anxiety about late deliveries and angry customers.

The Management Meeting. Leaders who are successful in developing their team into an effective problem-solving and decision-making group certainly are preventing many conflicts. For today's problems, left unresolved, often cause tomorrow's conflicts. Also, in effective management meetings, policies get formulated and rules established; and, because the purpose of policies and rules is providing people with a clear understanding of what can and cannot be done, they serve to reduce "unacceptable" behaviors, which obviously prevent future conflicts.

In my own organization, for example, the management team recently made a group decision that has effectively eliminated certain frequently occurring conflicts in the past. We adopted a policy of flexible schedules, or "flextime," that gives all employees discretion to choose when they come to work, when they leave, and how much time they spend for lunch, provided they put in a 40-hour work week. That one policy has prevented a lot of conflicts and misunderstandings.

While the same policy would not fit all organizations, it illustrates how decisions made by management groups can serve the function of prevention of conflicts.

The Preventive I-Message. A variant of the confrontive I-Message is the "Preventive I-Message," a simple assertion of what you need or want. Usually, this type of I-Message is employed *before* any unacceptable behavior might occur—hence, the term Preventive I-Message. The assertion "I'm going to need complete privacy today to get my report done" communicates a special need of yours and serves notice that you want to prevent interruptions, which today would be particularly unacceptable and perhaps lead to conflicts with your group members. Again note how much more effective such a Preventive I-Message is than a You-Message: "You are not to interrupt me today under any circumstances."

The Self-Disclosure I-Message. Another form of I-Message communicates (discloses) what you think, believe, or value. Such messages often prevent conflict because they let people know where you stand. The message "I strongly believe that courtesy on the phone is a prerequisite for good customer relationships" clearly discloses what you value, which informs group members that discourtesy will be unacceptable to you. Now that they know where you stand, they can avoid possible conflict with you by a conscious effort to be courteous in phone calls with customers.

While these methods and skills do prevent many conflicts, it would be naive for any leader to hope that conflicts will never develop in relationships with others. In fact, as I have said, a good case can be made for the position that the *absence* of conflict may be symptomatic of an organization or group that is not functioning effectively—not growing, changing, adapting, improving, or creatively meeting new challenges. Experience convinces me that the *number* of conflicts in groups (including families) is not at all indicative of how "healthy" they are. The true index is whether the conflicts get resolved and by what method they get resolved. Whether they get resolved is critical because some leaders have a tendency to avoid resolution of conflict by walking away from it, hoping that the conflict will go away by itself.

I have heard executives proudly describe their groups or organizations: "We're just a big happy family around here—we get along, no problems." I am always suspicious of such leaders, as I am suspicious of husbands and wives who say, "We've been married for twenty years and we've never had a fight." Usually that means that their conflicts are not allowed to surface and be faced.

Some people actually fear conflict. They feel anxious and uncomfortable with conflicts, so they take the attitude of "peace at any price." They don't want to rock the boat; it's essential for them to "keep their skirts clean." Therefore, they avoid getting involved in anything that smacks of conflict. But they pay a price for this posture, because the results of avoiding conflict are quite predictable:

1. Resentments Build Up. This is true in all relationships, not just leader-member relationships. When conflicts remain unresolved, resentments gradually build up. Then, maybe months later, when a minor problem crops up, all the accumulated resentment erupts explosively, usually far out of proportion to the particular problem of the moment.

2. Feelings Get Displaced onto Other People or Things. The leader who does not resolve conflicts at the office may go home and displace his resentments onto his family— complaining to his wife, barking at the kids, or shouting at the dog.

3. Griping, Backbiting, Gossiping, General Discontent. One of the surest signs of unresolved conflicts in organizations is an atmosphere of excessive griping, behind-the-back criticism, or incessant gossiping.

The point is that you cannot afford to run away from conflicts, because resentment will build up, feelings will get displaced, or there will be symptoms of the discontent and hostility people experience when conflicts exist among the people with whom they work. Conflicts should be brought out in the open and resolved, not shoved under the rug or suppressed.

If conflicts are inevitable in most organizations and groups, how do they occur and who gets involved?

Some conflicts occur when I-Messages fail to influence the other person to change unacceptable behavior to acceptable behavior. And you can expect even good I-Messages to fail sometimes, usually when the other person has strong needs to continue the particular behavior or strong fears about changing, as in these situations:

In one organization I know, the president felt he was not kept informed frequently enough about the progress (or lack of it) in one of the company's divisions, research and development. The president confronted the division head with appropriate I-Messages and received assurance that the situation would be corrected. Months later, still no progress report. Another confrontation was no more successful. Obviously, there was some conflict between the needs of the president and the needs of the division head. Later, the conflict was faced in a conference between the two of them. The president learned that the division head had strong resistance to consulting with the president, centered around fears of either being criticized or having the president make substantive changes in the division head's "pet" project, about which he had strong proprietary interests.

In a small law office, the partners became dissatisfied with the way their offices were being cleaned. I-Messages influenced the maintenance worker to be more thorough for a short time, but a week later he reverted back to his old sloppy habits.

The accountant in a manufacturing plant was confronted about her monthly reports being overly complicated and difficult to interpret, yet months later the president could see little improvement.

In management meetings, too, conflict often emerges just when the group works down to the decision-making step in the problem-solving process. One solution is favored by most of the group members, but one or two members strongly resist that solution and prolonged discussion fails to bring about agreement. Recently I saw such a conflict occur within a management team over the very controversial issue of changing from a 40-hour to a 37½-hour work week.

As a leader you can count on becoming involved in conflicts with a wide variety of people: with your total management team, with only one or two of your group members, with your own supervisor, with the head of another department or division. And finally, you may get drawn into a conflict between two of your own group members.

To summarize what I have said about conflicts: they can be serious, unpleasant, and disruptive; they are inevitable in human relationships; some can be prevented by using effective communication skills; they occur in organizations that are growing and changing; they often emerge when I-Messages fail; they often surface at the time your group is trying to finalize a decision during problem-solving; and you may get involved in conflicts with any number of people with whom you are associated in the organization.

THREE DIFFERENT METHODS FOR RESOLVING CONFLICTS

Resolving conflicts is not understood by most leaders—it looks complex and they feel unprepared and ill equipped for it. Conflicts frighten them, produce tension and anxiety (and depression). Or conflicts simply make them angry and resentful toward the people whose behavior generated controversy or disagreement. Some leaders view conflicts as a symptom of their incompetence, a sure sign of some impending defeat.

Such reactions are not surprising, for they are rooted in past experiences, going all the way back to childhood. For most people, getting into fights with siblings and peers when they were kids—or with parents, teachers, school administrators—provoked fear and anger or brought on rapid heartbeat, yelling and screaming, fractured relationships. Past conflicts for most people turned into power struggles in which someone was bound to win and someone to lose. Inevitably the relationship suffered.

This universal negative experience with conflict is easily explained. Throughout their lives, in most of their relationships, people have employed (or have had used on them) *win-lose methods* of conflict resolution, which invariably meant someone losing and someone winning. Actually, there are two win-lose methods, and most people employ either one or the other:

METHOD I: I win, you lose

METHOD II: You win, I lose

Virtually unknown to leaders and rarely employed in organizations, a third method exists for resolving conflicts between people: the *No-lose Method*. Method III, as we also call it in our L.E.T. course, is easy to understand and we have learned how to teach leaders to use it in all kinds of situations involving conflicts with others. Acquiring a high level of competence with Method III is not easy; it requires practice. Its use requires leaders to learn how to use the communication skills (listening *and* assertive skills), and it challenges leaders to discard some firmly entrenched habitual patterns of relating to others.

The remainder of this chapter explains the two win-lose methods—exactly how they work and what outcomes can be expected when they are employed. In the next chapter, the No-lose Method will be explained and illustrated.

HOW METHODS I AND II WORK

Put yourself in the role of Fred Lee, a department manager with five supervisors reporting to you. You receive a memo from one of them, Tom Shane, informing you of his intention to fire Frank, one of his workers. You don't understand this; Frank has been with the organization for many years and has been an excellent worker. You confront Tom with your puzzlement and express your wish that he seriously reconsider his decision. Tom refuses and again says he is convinced that Frank must be fired.

There is the conflict. Now, if you tell Tom he could not fire Frank, that he must try to work things out with him, you would be using the Method I approach in conflict resolution: you win, Tom loses. Method I can be represented by the following diagram:

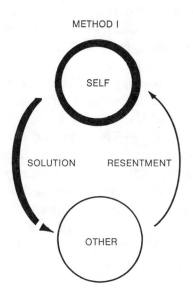

METHOD I

SELF

SOLUTION   RESENTMENT

OTHER

In Method I you impose a solution that enables you to get your way at the expense of the other person not getting his. Your needs are satisfied, the other person's needs are not. Your solution prevails, his is rejected. Inevitably, the loser feels resentment toward the winner because it seems unfair to him. Using the terminology of social exchange theory, this is an "inequitable social exchange" with the benefits tipped heavily in your favor. And, as I shall later point out in detail, you can expect negative reactions that will be destructive to your relationship with Tom.

Method I, obviously, a win-lose conflict-resolution method, goes by several other names:

Unilateral decision-making

Authoritarian decision-making

Leader-centered decision-making

Domination

Instead of using Method I, suppose, after you confront Tom with your objections to firing Frank and hear his resistance to changing his point of view, you then reluctantly give up and give in. Although you feel you are right, you let Tom have his way. Perhaps you are afraid to lose his friendship, or you hate to get into a serious conflict. Or maybe you want to be seen by Tom as a nice guy. For whatever reason, you let Tom win, and you lose. His needs get satisfied, yours do not. His solution prevails, making it feel like an "inequitable social exchange" to you. You feel resentful toward Tom. Later, as we shall see, Tom will feel the consequences of your resentment.

With this approach you would be using Method II, the direct opposite of Method I, yet a win-lose method, too. Often it goes under the names of

Permissiveness

Soft management

Employee-centered decision-making

Subordination

Laissez-faire leadership

Method II can be represented by this diagram:

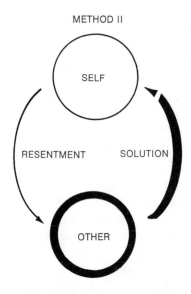

METHOD II

SELF

RESENTMENT   SOLUTION

OTHER

Perhaps it has occurred to you that Methods I and II, both in the past and currently, have sharply polarized the thinking of many people who teach or write about leadership in management or organizational development. Articles and books have appeared by the hundreds by writers who take the strong position that "leaders must make final decisions," that "leaders must lead," "decision-making is the prerogative of the boss," "arbitrary decisions are inevitable," "authority must be used though exercised wisely," "leaders must be fair but firm," "nice managers don't win ball games," and other variations on the theme. Recent advocacy for leaders exercising their authority in decision-making undoubtedly comes as a backlash to several decades of the so-called "human relations movement," with its emphasis on employee participation, nonauthoritarian leadership, group decisions, employee-oriented supervision, attention to the needs of workers, treating subordinates as equals, and so on.

The opponents of the "human relations" school of thought have attacked its proponents on the grounds that they advocate "permissive leadership," "soft management," or a "laissez-faire" posture toward employees. In short, they often equate "human relations" with Method II, where the subordinates' needs get met at the expense of the leader's needs not getting met. Naturally, the advocates of authoritarian leadership would say, "It is paramount that the leader's needs be met, and so a leader has to use authority." But then this sounds suspiciously like Method I.

I take the position that *neither* school of thought is correct, that leaders *necessarily* pay a terrible price when they use a method that gets their needs satisfied at the expense of group members not getting their needs satisfied (Method I), as well as when they use a method that sacrifices their needs in favor of the needs of group members (Method II). Exactly what price must leaders pay for either posture? I will deal with Method II first, because the outcomes and effects of Method I are considerably more complex and require an in-depth analysis of the concept of *power*.

THE PRICE OF USING METHOD II

Who enjoys losing conflicts? Deprivation of your needs in favor of the satisfaction of another's doesn't ever feel fair. You'll be resentful and angry and certainly not feel very good about that relationship. Or you'll carry your feelings home with you and gripe to your spouse. You may even sulk and be unpleasant with the person who became the winner. More serious, you might develop insecurities about your job because you are afraid that the other person has won at the expense of not doing what is required to meet the goals of the organization. Leaders who give in to the wants and wishes of their group members in the cause of having happy and contented workers usually pay the price of developing a group that is not productive and "task-oriented." And remember, effective leaders must have groups that have *both* good "human relations" and high productivity.

The same is true with parents who are permissive with their children—and teachers with students. In homes with permissive parents, kids become inconsiderate, selfish, uncooperative, freeloading, and often totally unmanageable. The classrooms of permissive teachers are invariably chaotic—full of aggressive, noisy, and boisterous kids—making it next to impossible for the kids to learn or the teacher to teach.

Method II, in the long run, is self-defeating, which accounts for the fact that most leaders do not really like being permissive. It's just that some fall into it because it seems a better choice than being autocratic, and they know of no third alternative.

THE COSTS OF USING POWER

To get people to accept and carry out a decision they are opposed to—one that gives them the feeling they're losing—invariably requires *power*—either employing it or threatening to employ it. But what is power? How does it work? And how does a person get it in the first place?

First, a person has power when he or she possesses the

means to deprive others of something they need. The actual exercise of power involves some action that causes others to behave in a certain way despite their opposition to it—makes them do something they otherwise would not do. The term psychologists generally use for the "means to deprive others" is "punishment" because to be deprived of something we want very much is felt as punishing. "If you don't do what I want, then I will deprive you of something you need." The use of this source of power is *coercive,* for the recipient feels coerced into compliance with the leader's solution.

Another source of power is derived from possessing the means to provide others with what they need in exchange for compliance to the desires of the person with the power. "If you do what I want, then I will give you something you need." Compliance in this case is achieved by the promise of benefits or *rewards* or the fear of being deprived of the rewards.

Punishments and rewards, then, are the sources from which a person's power is derived. This is the specific definition of power employed throughout this book. Later I will differentiate between power and two other important concepts: influence and authority.

For power to work for you in a relationship with another, that person must be relatively *dependent* on you for the satisfaction of his or her needs. To get your group members to carry out a decision you have unilaterally made yet one they are opposed to, they must not only want very much whatever rewards you offer but also be relatively unable to get those rewards elsewhere. The more dependent your group members are on you for getting their needs satisfied, the more power you will have.

For example, during a period of high unemployment caused by a business recession, employees are much more dependent on their employer for getting wages or salaries, obviously because it would be difficult for them to find jobs elsewhere.

An older employee who has built up a lot of retirement credit over the years will be very dependent on her employer because if she resigned before retirement age she would lose all the money put away for retirement income.

If one of your group members has unique skills that are very useful for your particular organization but not salable in any others, his dependence on you might be very great.

Another necessary condition for power to work is that your group members have a certain amount of *fear;* they must be kept afraid that you in fact will punish them if they don't comply with a decision they don't like. Having the means to deprive or punish someone is one thing, but actually doing it is another. *The existence of a leader's power is made visible only through its use.* The more frequently it is used, the stronger will be the group members' fear of their leader. Conversely, their fear will diminish if you don't exercise your power at all.

In my experience, most leaders are not aware of these conditions that are necessary for power to work. If they were, they would understand the costly price they must pay for using power: having dependent and submissive group members who are kept in a state of fear and anxiety. Paradoxical as it may seem, while most leaders firmly believe they need power to be effective, few would ever say they wanted group members who are dependent and fearful. Yet that is exactly what is required, if power is to work.

Perhaps now it is clear why leaders in so many organizations in our society find they can no longer rely heavily on power. Either they don't have it in the first place, or they have much too little. Because over the years, the power differential between leaders and those they are expected to lead has been steadily decreasing in most organizations, as a result of many different factors, such as:

1. The emergence of unions and trade associations, which have greatly restricted the possibility of coercive actions of employers toward employees.

2. Increased job mobility—it is now easier for workers to find jobs in other organizations.

3. The difficulty of firing people in civil service positions, such as schoolteachers and government employees.

4. The increase in number of highly skilled workers brought about by an ever advancing technology, thus making it costly for organizations to train new employees after firing old ones.

5. The trend toward transferring some of the power of managers and supervisors to personnel departments—e.g., wage and salary administration, employee benefits, grievance procedures, and so on.

In some kinds of organizations, to be sure, the power of leaders is carefully prescribed and seriously limited by by-laws or by a constitution. In many organizations leaders are elected by the members, and if they become autocratic and coercive they can be removed or impeached. In organizations whose members are volunteers—service clubs, fraternal organizations, civic groups, political parties, and the like—leaders have almost no power.

In summary, Method I requires leaders to use power in order to coerce people into doing something they don't want to do. But power is derived from the possession of the means to reward or punish people into compliance. The trouble is, for power to work with people, they have to be very dependent on their leaders and be afraid of them, too. In most organizations, however, subordinates are not all that dependent or fearful—they have considerable power on their side.

HOW PEOPLE REACT TO POWER

All but ignored by those who defend the use of Method I in resolving conflicts is what coercive power actually does to people and their relationships. Nobody likes to lose; nobody enjoys relationships that tip the balance of benefits in favor of the other person; nobody wants to be coerced into doing something that results in deprivation. No wonder power provokes such a variety of reactions in people—fighting it, avoiding it, defending against it, or trying to nullify its effects on them. The technical term for such reactions to power is "coping mechanisms."

Reduction in Upward Communication

One of the most damaging effects of power on organizational effectiveness is the marked reduction in upward communication—from group members to their leaders. Leaders who frequently use reward and punishment complain, not surprisingly, that they never know what is going on. "Nobody tells me anything." "I'm the last person to know."

Anyone who has worked for a Method I leader knows why. Subordinates of authoritarian leaders are reluctant to reveal problems because they know there is a good chance of having their boss's unilateral solutions imposed on them. They don't feel safe to bring facts to their boss's attention because they fear unpleasant consequences may ensue. "What the boss doesn't know won't hurt me" is the attitude of people afraid of their boss.

Not only does power reduce the *frequency* of upward communication; it also affects *accuracy*. In relationships with leaders who rely heavily on reward and punishment, group members selectively send messages that they think will only bring rewards, avoiding messages that might invite punishment. "Tell the boss what he wants to hear" governs their behavior. The name of the game becomes "Tell him anything to avoid punishment" or "Don't get caught."

Power most seriously produces counterproductive behavior when coercive behavior of the leader tangibly reduces the effectiveness of a group member, as in this situation:

Gloria sends urgent appeals to her division head asking for information she needs to solve problems and make decisions in her department. Often these requests are ignored by her boss for several days or even weeks, causing delays in making important decisions and seriously reducing the effectiveness of her department. Gloria is afraid to confront her boss because in the past when she has had conflicts with her, Gloria always comes out the loser, having to accept solutions that are not workable. Gloria now spends a lot of time putting all such requests in written memos, so she'll have documentation to defend herself in case the performance of her department is criticized.

Obviously Gloria's method of coping in this situation is counterproductive. Instead of confronting her boss honestly, which she fears, she becomes defensive.

Apple-Polishing and Other Ingratiating Reactions

A not uncommon coping mechanism for group members to deal with power-wielding leaders is to behave so they'll "get on the good side" of their leader. The purpose is to seek the leader's approval on some basis other than the one in which the power differential is based. Flattery and "apple-polishing" flourish in groups and organizations with leaders who use power frequently. People soon learn that leaders do not mete out rewards and punishments equally to all group members—leaders have favorites just as teachers have "teacher's pets."

Apple-polishing carries two risks: flattery may be discovered by the boss for what it is, and the apple-polisher is usually disliked by other group members.

A variation of apple-polishing occurs so frequently in organizations it has earned a special name for its users— "yes-men" (I'll ignore the obvious sexism in the label). It refers to people who consciously make an effort to agree with the opinions of the one in power. While this coping mechanism may sometimes work, it carries the risk of being objectionable to the leader and odious to other group members.

A third method people have been known to use to ingratiate themselves to the power holder is deliberately displaying their attractiveness—physical or intellectual. Sexploitation is common in organizations, even though it has long proved counterproductive and perilous. Similarly, people who flaunt their intellectual prowess to gain approval generally irritate more often than ingratiate.

Destructive Competitiveness and Rivalry

The most predictable reaction to coercive power is heightened competitiveness and rivalry between group members. In extreme cases it causes tattling, backbiting, cheating, covering up, gossiping, or character defamation. The power struggles and interpersonal battles of the "executive suite" and the "corporate jungle" are not just proverbial and fictional. The roots of such common behaviors can be traced back to the family, where children invariably react to the coercive power of parental rewards and punishments by lying, tattling, belittling, and blaming their brothers and sisters—euphemistically called "sibling rivalry." A leader's use of heavy doses of and punishments, whether in the family or in ions, generates strong competition among members to snare all the rewards and artfully dodge all the punishments.

The formula is simple: "If I can make others look bad, I may look better by comparison; if I can blame others, I may be able to avoid punishment."

Competition and rivalry between the members of a group are the antithesis of the cooperation and team play needed in an effective management group. This is why "team building" is an empty abstraction for a group whose leader controls with power.

Submission and Conformity

For reasons not entirely understood, some people have learned to cope with power by submission and conformity. They choose obedience and compliance, passively knuckling under to the person with greater power. The formula is: "I will get more rewards by doing exactly what I'm told to do, but nothing more."

Some leaders, it's true, may find the prospect of having obedient subordinates most appealing. Imagine, subordinates who do exactly what they're told to do! The trouble is: these people usually have to be told what to do or they won't do much. They are weak in initiative and low in creativity. Their leaders must spend inordinate amounts of time giving them explicit directions and solving problems for them when things go wrong or the unexpected occurs. Executives have complained to me about subordinates who demand of them, "You call the shots," or "You just tell me what to do, boss, and I'll make sure it gets done." The problem with this is that bosses often don't know exactly how a task should be done. Even worse, they may think they know, but it turns out they don't. The plant manager of a midwestern company making hydraulic pumps reported this conversation with one of his foremen:

Manager: Do you know that you've made this part upside down?

Foreman: Hell, yes, I know it's upside down. I tried to tell them upstairs, but there wasn't anybody listening. So orders are orders—we make it upside down.

Manager: You knew it was wrong, huh.

Foreman: Yeah. The only thing is, I'm going to make damn sure I'm not around here to hold the sack when the old boy finds out it doesn't work.

The foreman's "obedience" was obviously counterproductive in this case, as conformity often is. Most leaders don't really want submissive group members, and this comes up in many complaints I have heard from managers:

"These damned people don't know how to take responsibility."

"Why don't they take any initiative?"

"I don't know the answers to all the damned problems out there!"

"What we need is somebody who can carry out a job independently."

"They come to me with problems they could solve themselves."

Rebellion and Defiance

The opposite of submission and obedience is rebellion and defiance. Have you ever known people whose habitual reaction to power is to dig in their heels and resist being coerced? Or people who, when told by an autocratic leader what they must do, turn around and rebelliously do the opposite? These are common coping mechanisms, probably learned in early childhood in response to parental or teacher power.

A variation of this pattern shows up in group members

whose response to their superior's ideas or suggestions is automatic resistance and disagreement. Rebellion and defiance reactions are motivated by a strong need for defense against being coerced or controlled. It is a protective posture, often accompanied by suspicion or distrust of anyone with power.

Resistance by rebellious group members frustrates and irritates others who want to move ahead and get the problem solved. Resistant members slow a group down because their arguments and disagreements must be dealt with somehow. And because rebellion is consistent, others see through it and recognize that it is rebellion against the leader's power rather than disagreement with the leader's ideas—which weakens a group's functioning.

Forming Alliances and Coalitions

Well documented in studies of organizational behavior is the tendency for people to seek alliances or form coalitions to try to balance the power advantage of coercive leaders over their group members. "In union there is strength" is the underlying principle of this coping mechanism. Children do this with parents: "Let's make an agreement that we'll all hold out for going to Disneyland Saturday." Students do it with teachers: "If everyone complains about the long homework assignments, maybe the teacher will shorten them."

Through informal interactions with each other, members of work groups join together and develop "norms" that protect them against unilateral action of their managers: productivity norms (what constitutes a "fair day's work"), quality standards, length of lunch break, etc. Nonconformity may be punished by ridicule or harassment. A lone individual is at a disadvantage in defending against coercive power; bargaining as a member of a group usually is much more effective. This principle led to trade unions and the consequent reduction of the power differential between employer and employees.

Perhaps it is inevitable that coercive power generates the very forces that eventually will combat it and bring about a more equitable balance of power. Power sows the seeds for its own destruction. "Uneasy rests the head that wears the crown."

Withdrawing and Escaping

Some people cope with coercive power by finding ways to remove themselves from the relationship—either physically or psychologically. Group members may avoid as many interactions as they can with their authoritarian leader—"stay out of his way" and "keep out of sight" as much as possible. This coping mechanism can be observed in group meetings where some members deliberately refrain from speaking out for fear of being judged, put down, or told what to do.

Research studies have shown that coercive supervisors have higher turnover rates. Most people, if given the opportunity, will leave a job in which they are strongly controlled and dominated by a power-wielding boss. I once knew an executive who was known by all of his subordinates and associates as an authoritarian and highly evaluative boss. Over a period of less than three years, four of his secretaries resigned because of the way he treated them.

THE EFFECT OF POWER ON THE LEADER

Equally important are the effects of power on the person who employs it. What power does to leaders who use it is a topic seldom discussed in books and articles about management and leadership. Yet I am convinced that power hurts the one that uses it as much as those on whom it is used. If more leaders understood this, most of them would be dissuaded from using power in their relationships.

The Cost of Time

Because power generates so much resistance in people and provokes them into challenging leaders who use it, it is understandable why leaders must spend a great amount of time and effort dealing with such reactions. Yet leaders often defend their use of power on the grounds that it takes *less* time than other nonpower methods of problem-solving or conflict resolution. This is a half-truth. While the act of *making* a Method I decision can take less time than a group decision, inordinate amounts of time are often required to achieve *acceptance* of a decision made unilaterally. The president of a company in which I served as a consultant for over a decade made this admission:

"When I was using Method I to resolve all the conflicts, I prided myself on being a person who could make decisions quickly. The trouble was, it often took ten times as long to overcome all the resistance to my decisions as it did to make them. I had to spend too much time 'selling' my decisions— getting other people to buy them. In the long run, this consumed a lot of my time."

I have observed executives taking hours to compose a long and involved memorandum to justify some unilateral decision; they knew full well how much resistance would be generated among the people who were expected to implement the decision.

The Cost of Enforcement

Because people usually have low motivation to implement a decision that is imposed on them—especially one that makes them feel like losers—enforcement of unilateral decisions is difficult as well as time-consuming. Nowhere is this more apparent than in schools, where teachers, based on their own estimates, spend as much as 75 percent of their classroom time enforcing Method I rules made unilaterally by their administrators. "Playing Policeman" is what teachers call it.

In other organizations many leaders have to play policeman, too. When there is little acceptance of a rule or policy, people find all kinds of devious ways to avoid compliance—passive resistance, "forgetting," lying, or falsifying records. Policing employees makes the cost of Method I high.

The Cost of Alienation

One of the hidden costs for leaders who rely heavily on power is that they become alienated from their group members. Personal relationships with their own people inevitably deteriorate, which explains why so many leaders say they feel "alone at the top." Two factors are at work. First, group members certainly won't feel warm toward a leader whom they fear and whose use of power makes them feel hostility. Secondly, leaders who control and coerce with rewards and punishment recognize that if they do develop close relationships with any of their subordinates they might be accused of "playing favorites." To avoid this, authoritarian leaders usually make it a rule never to get too close to subordinates, which in the military is termed "getting buddy-buddy."

No wonder authoritarian leaders in organizations have so few close friendships with the people who work for them. This is an unfortunate price to pay for being in a leadership position—one of the hidden costs of using power.

The Cost of Stress

It is a widely accepted idea that executives and administrators find their jobs stressful—often damaging to their physical and mental health. We are led to believe that being a leader invariably brings tension, anxiety, and worry. And the inevitable price of leadership, so we are told, is high blood pressure, a coronary, an ulcer, or alcoholism. Could it be that high stress so often goes with leadership not because of the responsibilities of the leader's unique position but because most leaders use power? Could power make its users "sick"?

A strong case can be made for the validity of that notion. Because people who use power in their relationships must constantly maintain a high level of personal vigilance, for a variety of reasons: they must vigorously enforce the rules they impose on others; they often feel they must be wary of people acquiring more power than themselves; they need to be suspicious of people who might undermine their "authority"; and, because people usually are not completely honest with those who hold the power, leaders probably grow to distrust others.

These would be sufficient producers of stress and tension for leaders, but there are others. Using power—winning at the expense of others losing—usually produces guilt. Then there is anxiety over how and when the losers might retaliate. Also, leaders who use power often get locked in to a perpetual search to acquire even more power—they learn to play the "power game" or they become "power mad." Perhaps these are the consequences of power Lord Acton had in mind when he wrote: "Power corrupts, and absolute power corrupts absolutely."

My own experience as a consultant and counselor to hundreds of leaders convinces me that those who play the power game create their own "psychological hell" of distrust, suspicion, paranoia, vigilance, tension, guilt, and anxiety. By using power, they manufacture their own "sickness," physical and mental.

The Cost of Diminishing Influence

Contrary to the common belief that the acquisition of power gives a leader *more* influence, power actually makes a leader *lose* influence over group members. To understand this paradox, one must remember that in the English language one word, "authority," is used for two entirely different concepts:

1. *Authority* derived from knowledge, experience, expertise, training.

2. *Authority* derived from the power to reward and punish in order to enforce obedience.

Using the first meaning we say, "I consulted an authority," "He speaks authoritatively," or, "She is an authority in her field." The exercise of this kind of authority involves teaching and the giving of facts and knowledge, with the desired outcome being the *influencing* of another. Call this Authority$_K$ (for Knowledge).

Using the second meaning, we say, "The boss has authority over his subordinates," "Don't assign responsibility without giving a person the authority needed to carry it out," "Who is in authority here?" "They don't respect his authority," "They challenged his authority." Exercising this kind of authority involves using power, with the desired outcome being the *coercing* of another. Call this Authority$_p$ (for Power).

When a leader employs Authority$_p$, group members

are seldom *influenced;* they are *coerced.* But they might be influenced were the leader to choose to use only Authority$_K$.

Why does the use of Authority$_p$ bring about a reduction in the potency of Authority$_K$? Power, as we have pointed out, often fosters resistance (active or passive), withdrawal and rebellion, in which case the power obviously does not produce compliance.

There is a third and distinctly different kind of authority —not exactly derived from the possession of expertise and knowledge nor from the coercive power of rewards and punishment. It is, in fact, a second type of influence that leaders commonly and successfully employ with group members. Call it Authority$_J$ (for Job Definition).

A jumbo jet is approaching the runway to land at Los Angeles International Airport. The captain rather forcefully and loudly says, "Flaps down," and without hesitation the copilot pulls a lever that lowers the flaps. A few seconds later the captain says, "Airspeed." Again the copilot responds by returning the message, "Airspeed 140."

Did the captain use his Authority$_p$—coercive power? Not in the least. Yet the copilot complied (or obeyed). Did the captain use his Authority$_K$—giving advice, facts, experience? Again, no. Yet obviously the captain was successful in influencing the copilot to do exactly what he wanted him to do. What was the source of his influence?

No doubt it is already apparent that the captain's influence is derived from the fact that *he is the captain.* That's his job, and part of the job description (or job definition) is that when he is landing the aircraft he tells the copilot when to lower the flaps and when to read aloud the airspeed indicator. The copilot understands this and accepts it; and it is part of his own job definition that when the captain says, "Flaps down," he puts them down without delay. Same for calling out the airspeed.

Authority$_J$ is "sanctioned" authority—a second kind of influence over others. The key to the success of Authority$_J$ is that the recipients of the influence attempt understand and accept the "right" of the influencer to direct their behavior. Other familiar examples of Authority$_J$:

An executive calls out to her secretary, "Madge, take a letter to Mr. Howard Feingold!"

The president of the PTA council at the start of their meeting shouts, "Stand and sing the national anthem!"

The chairman of the board of directors forcefully raps the gavel on the table and orders, "The meeting will come to order. Take your seats, ladies and gentlemen!"

The foreman of a packing crew whistles loudly to get his people's attention and says, "Put more string around those boxes and pull 'em tighter!"

In contrast to power (Authority$_p$), this type of "legitimate" authority resides in the structured relationship between jobs or positions in an organization. It is often called "legitimated authority," and stems from expectations of the roles people have been assigned. Generally, an attempt to influence behavior based on Authority$_J$ is not likely to generate resistance and resentment because everyone understands and accepts that such influence is necessary in order to get the job done, whatever that job might be.

Authority$_p$ is often arbitrary, while Authority$_J$ is not. The latter is what is expected—the price one pays for organizational effectiveness. And seldom does its use alone create resentment and hostility.

However, leaders who frequently use their coercive

power (Authority p) will find that the influence derived from their Authority j is likely to provoke the same amount of resistance and resentment as power. Predictably, there is a carry-over of feelings from one situation in which a person has been coerced to the next situation in which the leader is only influencing.

A supervisor uses coercive power to get compliance to an arbitrary and unilateral decision he has made: "If you guys don't quit your talking, you're going to work overtime tonight and I mean it. So no more talking, OK?" Later, the supervisor (using the legitimate authority of his position) tells his workers, "OK, stop now and check with each other to find out how far each of you has progressed." The men stop work and stand silently looking down at their benches, but don't check with each other. "What the hell is the matter?" asks the supervisor. They answer (with a smirk), "But you told us we couldn't talk."

Such retaliatory behavior is not uncommon when leaders resort to power (or "pull rank," as it is called in the military).

Have you ever observed subordinates responding even to a legitimated influence attempt with such remarks as:

"Whatever you say, boss."

"Yes, sir, if you say so."

"You're the boss."

"Right away, sir."

The feelings beneath these messages are carry-overs from the leader's prior use of Authority p.

One final caution: if Authority j influence attempts are couched in words that communicate to group members that the leader feels he or she has superior status or has the attitude that obedience is desired, then those attempts to influence behavior will be felt by the recipients more as coercion than as an influence attempt. When leaders actually believe they are superior and infinitely more worthy than their group members, they can't help but act arrogantly toward their people because it is next to impossible in enduring relationships for people to hide their true feelings.

IX. THE NO-LOSE METHOD: TURNING CONFLICT INTO COOPERATION

ALTHOUGH most people know from personal experience that the two win-lose methods of conflict resolution carry a high risk of damaging relationships and reducing organizational effectiveness, these continue to be the methods of choice for most leaders. While there may be a number of explanations for this, two seem most probable: people have had little or no personal experience with any other approach to conflict resolution, and, in the minds of most people, having the greatest influence is equated with possessing the most power.

Most children were brought up in families in which one or both parents administered frequent and liberal doses of rewards and punishments to make their kids do what the adult decided they should do. A recent nationwide study of violence in families found that 80 percent of the parents said they used ordinary means of physical punishment, such as spanking and slapping. Nearly 30 percent of the parents had committed a violent act against their children for which they could have been arrested for assault! Likewise, in schools, rewards and punishments have always been the principal tools teachers have used to get "discipline" in the classroom. That practice hasn't changed much for several hundred years, which is a source of some amazement to me. This means that by the time youngsters are ready to move into adulthood, very few have been exposed to any other model of adult-child conflict resolution except the one in which adults use power to enforce obedience.

So, children get little opportunity to experience relationships with adults who use nonpower methods. All they experience is coercion and domination. Even if you ask youngsters, as I have, why authority and power failed to make them comply to teachers' and parents' demands, with amazing frequency they reply, "I guess they should have used *more.*"

No wonder nine out of ten people who have come to our L.E.T. classes over the past dozen years are so surprised to learn that there actually is a workable alternative to win-lose methods. And no wonder these leaders express such disbelief when confronted with the idea that they lose influence when they use power. In fact, most of them enroll in the L.E.T. course expecting to be taught how to use their power more cleverly or more wisely— certainly never expecting to be taught not to use it at all!

WHAT IS THE NO-LOSE METHOD?

The alternative to the win-lose methods of resolving conflicts is a third method by which nobody loses— hence the name No-lose Method. If you will recall our definition of an effective leader, it is a person who has skills to meet the needs of his or her group members as well as the needs of the organization: "the effective leader must acquire the flexibility or sensitivity to know when and where to employ these quite diverse skills to achieve *mutual satisfaction of the needs of group members and the needs of the leader."* The No-lose Method does just that. It is a method producing a solution that brings *mutual need satisfaction.*

Because the win-lose orientation is so prevalent in our society, the first reaction most people have, when introduced to the No-lose Method, is that it seems new and strange—foreign to their experience. However, most people have much more experience with the No-lose Method than they think.

Two children get into a conflict about what to play. Melanie wants to play "house," but Michele wants to play with their miniature automobiles. Each tries unsuccessfully to persuade ("win over") the other. Finally, Michele offers this solution: "I'll play 'house' with you, if you play 'cars' with me now while its still light outside. When it gets dark, we'll go in my room and play 'house' until dinnertime. OK?" Melanie thinks for a second and says, "OK."

That's the No-lose Method! Kids use it all the time. They've probably been using it for as long as kids have been around.

A husband and wife go on a camping trip. A conflict develops over who is to prepare the meals. They talk about it and arrive at a solution acceptable to both: the husband agrees to handle the evening meal, provided the wife prepares the breakfast, so he'll have that time to get the fishing gear collected and placed in the boat. And they agree that each will get lunch on their own.

That, too, is the No-lose Method in action! Husbands and wives use it frequently, and in all kinds of conflicts. Also, friends commonly use the No-lose Method to work out amicable solutions to conflicts about such matters as which restaurant to go to, what time to start on a Sunday outing, where to go on a vacation together, what time to end an evening bridge game, who brings what food to a picnic, and so on.

Obviously, most people have a lot of experience with the No-lose Method. Then why is it so seldom used in boss-subordinate relationships? And in parent-child relationships? And in teacher-student relationships? It is because in these particular relationships there is an obvious power differential which doesn't usually exist in child-child, husband-wife, or friend-friend relationships. In these power is more or less balanced.

It is hard to escape this conclusion: when people possess power over others, they are very much inclined to use it. When they don't, they recognize that the No-lose Method is the only one they can use. Unless of course they give in to the other person (Method II), which nobody likes to do.

The No-lose Method (or Method III, as it is also called in our L.E.T. classes) thus requires that a leader, who usually does have more power than group members, makes a commitment *not* to use it. Instead, when conflict arises, the leader's attitude (paraphrased) is:

You and I have a conflict of needs. I respect your needs, but I must respect my own, too. I will not use my power over you so I win and you lose, but I cannot give in and let you win at the expense of my losing. So let's agree to search together for a solution that would satisfy your needs and also satisfy mine, so no one loses.

In diagram form Method III, the No-lose Method looks like this:

METHOD III

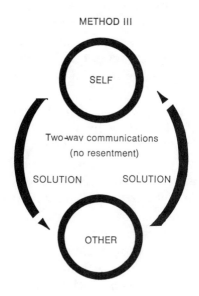

In the previous chapter, you will recall, I picked a specific conflict to illustrate Methods I and II. It was a conflict over firing an employee. That conflict was in fact resolved in real life by Method III. The tape-recorded dialogue of that meeting between Fred and Tom is presented below in full because it illustrates what goes on in a conflict-resolution meeting using the No-lose Method. The dialogue appears in the left column, my comments about the process on the right. Keep in mind that the No-lose Method is a special kind of problem-solving, so the process usually involves the same six steps as in problem-solving generally (see Chapter III):

I.   Identifying and defining the problem

II.   Generating alternative solutions

III. Evaluating the alternative solutions

IV.   Decision-making

V.   Implementing the decision

VI.   Following up to evaluate the solution

Fred: Good morning, Tom, how are you this morning?

Tom: Fine, Fred.

Fred: I asked you to come in to talk about Frank.

Tom: What do you mean? What about Frank?

Fred: I understand you want to terminate him.

Tom: Yes, you got my memo then. I'm recommending that we do terminate him.

Fred: I'd like to know more about this, Tom, what led up to this decision, why you feel this is necessary.

Fred sends an I-message here rather than one that would blame or judge Tom, such as "You shouldn't have made this decision" or "It's a bad decision."

Tom: I have several feelings about that, Fred. First, in my judgment he is a troublemaker and he has very definitely interfered with my getting the job done that you told me you wanted me to do. I took over this job—kind of a messy situation—and I have tried very hard to clean it up, but I can't do it as long as Frank is there. He is in my way, he doesn't follow instructions, he's just a troublemaker. But I guess I'm

a little concerned why
you are questioning my
authority.

Fred: You can't get the job
done that you're trying to
do because Frank is caus-
ing trouble with other
employees; and now I'm
adding to your trouble by
questioning your author-
ity.

Fred uses Active Listening to
communicate that he has understood Tom's feelings about his
dilemma.

Tom: Yes, I don't quite understand this. You put me
there to do a job and now
you're saying: "Wait a
minute, you're not doing
the job right." I think a
supervisor should have
the right to decide who is
going to work for him,
and my decision is that
Frank should go.

Fred: You feel it should be your
prerogative whether you
fire any of your em-
ployees or not.

Another good Active Listening
response.

Tom: Yeah, and I don't like to
have someone looking
over my shoulder; and I
think I have done my job
well. You'd probably
agree that I have cleaned
up a lot of things. We
have new procedures, we
are more efficient. I feel
pretty good about what
we've done.

Fred: You feel pretty good
about what you've ac-
complished but you feel

Fred continues to show empathy and understanding with an
Active Listening response.

I'm looking over your shoulder and second-guessing you.

Tom: I gather you're seriously questioning whether I should fire Frank or whether I have a right to fire him.

Fred: I don't question whether you have a right but I think we have a problem here, Tom, because Frank has been with us for twenty years and has had quite a satisfactory record. I think he might feel like some other employees perhaps feel, and as you would, too, if you were in the spot of being fired by me. Or if you had a long time with the organization and a new boss came in and perhaps there was a personality conflict, and the boss decided to fire you. I think you might feel badly about that, wouldn't you?

Here Fred defines the problem in terms of his own position on the matter.

Fred gets somewhat teachy and preachy here, which provokes defensiveness in Tom's next response.

Tom: As far as the point that we have a personality conflict, I would disagree.

Fred: I meant that only as an example. Let me retract that. You feel this is definitely not a personality conflict.

Tom: No, I think this is a situation where one rotten apple will spoil the barrel. I feel that if we leave Frank down here, his tendency to resist me is going to spread throughout the group and I'll lose my respect and the authority I have down there.

Tom defines the problem in terms of his own feelings and concerns.

Fred: I see, you feel that you need the respect which Frank might undermine, and that you need the authority to get things done here.

Fred does a good job of Active Listening to a new and deeper problem expressed by Tom. Often in problem solving the "presenting problem" gets defined into a more basic problem.

Tom: Right. I don't mind if a subordinate disagrees with me, but to disagree with me in front of a whole group! This is what Frank does and then the other people feel that they're free to do the same.

Fred: This is very interesting. It particularly bothers you if he disagrees with you in front of others. You feel this undermines your authority.

Tom: Right.

Fred: I'm a little puzzled here, Tom, about this authority and power that you feel you need.

Fred uses a door opener to invite Tom to elaborate on his need for power.

Tom: Well, I believe to get the job done—to clean up a situation like we have down here, you really have to let your subordinates know that you're the boss.

Fred: I see. Then you want them to feel that what you say goes, and you're making all the decisions.

Another effective Active Listening response.

Tom: Right. I don't like to have these decisions questioned because then I think this subordinate's whole attitude and morale is wrong.

Fred: I think I see a second problem emerging here, Tom. In addition to the problem that we started out with, I see now a problem that I would like to explore. This is the style of management you feel you need to exercise. It's true that some people run their departments authoritatively and do an effective job, but I think it has a lot of disadvantages which I would like to explore with you. I have some data which leads me to believe that if you have this authoritarian type of management, that you will have more turnover, that you will have a worse morale problem, that you won't get as good decisions be-

Fred identifies the second problem (and the more basic) and tries to separate it from the first. He then moves to a consulting role in an attempt to influence Tom to think of the consequences of his leadership style.

cause you don't get all the information. If you run a strict ship where people are afraid to tell you anything that you might not like, then they're not going to give you as much information. Without this information you can't make a good decision. But it sounds like you feel you can't run your department well without being an authoritarian boss. Seems to me these two problems are kind of interrelated. If Frank, a long-time employee, were fired, you wouldn't only have the problem of replacing him, and you know how hard it is to get good employees. He is well liked in the department. You think he has influence on the other men. I think that's evidence that the other guys kind of go along with him, and there is at least a possibility that some of the others might quit too. Either right away or as they could find another job that they liked better. If you lose several people down there, then what you're trying to accomplish couldn't be done. You are doing a good job of cleaning up a lot of things down there but you have to have good manpower to do it.

Tom: Right.

Fred: So now we have two problems here. I'd like to explore your management style with you as well as the Frank problem.

At this point Fred and Tom have completed only Step I of the problem-solving process: Identifying and Defining the Problem (in this case, two problems).

Tom: I see there is a difference in the way you're describing the supervision you use and the way I look at supervision, but I don't know what to do with a person like Frank.

Fred: This bothers you when he acts this way. Even if you wanted to adopt a different kind of management, you're kind of puzzled how you would go about this—what you'd do differently than you've done.

Tom: Yes.

Fred: I see this. It's something that a lot of people don't understand, Tom. I think perhaps, there are several sources of information on this. I hope I could be helpful to you. The Personnel Department can be very helpful to you also.

Fred moves into Step II, offering a possible solution to the second problem.

Tom: I'd like for you to talk to Frank. Would you be willing to talk to Frank?

Tom also gets into Step II, throwing out a solution to the first problem.

Fred: You'd like for me to talk with Frank alone. I'd be willing to, if . . .

Tom: I can't do anything with him.

Fred: Let's explore this further. You feel you can't get anyplace with him. My experience has taught me that it's worthwhile for the person with the problem to confront the person himself. Have you shared with him exactly what your feelings are and what the problem is?

Now Fred is into Step III, evaluating the alternate solution offered by Tom.

Fred is back in Step II, generating another solution to the first problem.

Tom: Well, I haven't sat down with him. I'm sure he knows what my feelings are—that I'm upset with him, but, no, I haven't sat down like you and I are discussing this. Are you suggesting that I have a formal kind of conference with him about this?

Fred: Yes.

Tom: I don't think that's going to do any good. I don't think he's the type of person to change—a person his age and his experience. But I guess I'd be willing to give it a try.

Tom is in Step III, evaluating Fred's alternative solution.

Fred: Now I would be willing, if you'd like, to sit in on something like that. I'd rather not undertake the job of working with him directly because I think

Fred offers another solution (Step II).

this would tend to undermine your relationship with him. Not your authority, there's a subtle difference here. But your relationship with him, which I think should be the primary one. But if I could simply be a facilitator and help you to understand him, and him to understand you, I'd be very happy to do this.

Tom: Well, what would you think of my trying it out first without you, and if I run into the difficulty that I think I will, then Frank and I could discuss this with you, because I don't know if I'm going to get anyplace with him.

Tom offers his alternative solution (Step II).

Fred: I think that's a good idea. I have another suggestion. You might think about it a little bit, and if we get together in the morning, we might do a little role playing—I'll pretend I'm Frank and we can practice this little session.

Now the process arrives at Step IV, Decision-making, as Fred agrees with Tom's solution. Fred moves into Step V, Implementing the solution, when he offers to role-play the conference with Tom.

Tom: That would help. Sort of have a rehearsal before I do it. I think that would help because I'm a little reluctant to go in there knowing what his attitude is, so you might have suggestions how I could do this.

Fred: OK. That's fine. We have the solution to one of our problems. The other one is trying to help you become a different type of manager. How do you think we should go about this?

Fred confirms the resolution of the first problem and moves back into the problem-solving process on the second problem: Tom's leadership style.

Tom: I understand we have a consultant who gives training programs of this type.

Tom generates a possible solution, followed by another solution from Fred in his next statement.

Fred: Yes, as a matter of fact we have had some supervisory training programs here before you came. We have some material on this—some of it is directly applicable. If you were to go over to Personnel Department and get some of this literature I think this would be helpful.

Tom: All right.

Decision-making occurs.

Fred: Also UCLA gives a course which they call Management Seminar which might be very helpful. Why don't I check into this for you and see if this is available? If you'd be willing to go there one night a week for the course.

Still Step II, generating another solution.

Tom: That's a good idea. I will certainly give it some thought. It was good to talk with you like this.

Tom agrees, and decision-making occurs again, with both agreeing with the solution.

This exchange illustrates what typically takes place in situations where Method III (or the No-lose Method) is successfully employed to resolve conflict:

1. The parties to the conflict move through the *problem-solving process,* at least through Step IV, Decision-making, and often beyond.

2. The conflict must get *defined and understood* in terms of both persons' needs, feelings, or concerns. You want your position to be understood, and you also want to be clear about the other person's position.

3. It is important that each person's needs, feelings, or concerns are expressed with *I-messages,* rather than blaming or judgmental You-messages, which usually impede the process.

4. *Active Listening* must be used because it communicates your acceptance and understanding of the other person's feelings. Only then will the other person feel willing to understand your feelings.

5. The initial "presenting problem" often turns into a deeper or *more basic problem,* which also has to be solved.

Unlike the two win-lose approaches, the No-lose Method is an "open-ended" approach to conflict resolution. Neither party to the conflict knows for sure what the ultimate solution will turn out to be—it's left open, it remains uncertain, it only emerges as an outcome from the six-step process (which, of course, *is* known). On the other hand, in the two win-lose methods, usually each (or just one) of the parties has in mind a preconceived solution, and the task is to use power to obtain compliance. This is why win-lose methods so often develop into power struggles over *competing solutions.* In short, Method III involves a *search* for a mutually acceptable solution, not a power struggle to get *compliance* with a predetermined solution.

Searching for a solution does not require power but creative thinking. Method III is like solving a puzzle:

"Let's put our heads together and see if we can come up with some solution that would meet the needs of both of us." "What could possibly resolve our conflict?" "We've got a problem to solve, so let's get creative!"

THE BENEFITS OF THE NO-LOSE METHOD

Understandably, leaders want to know the benefits of the No-lose Method before they make the effort to learn how to use it effectively. At the outset, I must emphasize that this method involves trade-offs: while it is easy enough to conceptualize, it is not easy to acquire competence in applying this method; it often takes more time to apply than the two win-lose methods; and there are special problems leaders will encounter when they use it. I will deal with these problems shortly. What about the benefits of the No-lose Method?

Increased Commitment to Carry Out the Decision

Everyone has had the experience of feeling a strong commitment to carry out a decision because of having had the chance to participate in formulating that decision. With a voice in the decision-making process, a person somehow has more motivation to implement the decision than if someone else unilaterally makes it. Psychologists call this commonsense idea the "Principle of Participation." It affirms the well-known phenomenon that when people participate in the problem-solving process and develop a mutually acceptable solution, they get the feeling it is "their" decision. They were responsible for helping to shape the decision, so they feel responsible for seeing that it works.

This heightened sense of responsibility or commitment usually means that less effort is required from the leader to enforce compliance—less need for the leader to play the policeman, as I pointed out earlier. Obviously, this yields a distinct saving of time for the leader and makes available more "productive work" time. A related benefit is greater organizational efficiency: when decisions are made, they get implemented; when conflicts are resolved, they stay resolved.

Higher-Quality Decisions

Method III enlists the creativity, experience, and brain-power of all parties involved in a conflict. It follows that this method would often produce high-quality decisions. And so it does. "Two heads are better than one" makes particularly good sense in conflict resolution because the needs of both (or all) parties must be accurately repre-sented. Also, with both parties participating in the solu-tion-generating, the odds are that they will brainstorm a larger number of creative solutions. Finally, the presence of both parties is necessary so each can judge which solu-tion best meets their needs.

It would be inconceivable to me, for example, to try to resolve a conflict between myself and one of my children (or my wife, or one of my group members) without their active participation—stating their needs and understand-ing mine, offering their solutions and hearing mine, evaluating each solution against their experience and con-sidering my evaluations based on my own experience. When I find myself in conflict with others, I want their help so we can find our way out of that conflict, with nobody losing. With such help I'll trust the quality of the solution much more than I'd trust one that I selected entirely on my own.

Warmer Relationships

One of the most predictable outcomes of the No-lose Method is that the parties to the conflict end up feeling good about each other. The resentment that usually follows either of the win-lose methods is absent in Method III. Instead, after a successful No-lose decision, there emerges a positive feeling of liking each other—yes, even loving each other. It probably comes from each person appreciating that the other was willing to be considerate of their needs and took the time to search for a solution that would make each happy. What better proof of caring?

Quicker Decisions

Have you ever experienced getting into a conflict with someone and then having that conflict go unresolved for weeks or months because you couldn't for the life of you figure out a solution? Then you found the courage to approach the person and invite him or her to join with you to try and resolve it. Much to your surprise, you reached an amicable and mutually acceptable solution in a matter of minutes.

This is not unusual. The No-lose Method often helps people in conflict get their feelings and needs out in the open, honestly face the issues, and explore possible solutions. Once started, the problem-solving process can lead quickly to a no-lose solution because it helps bring out a lot of data (facts *and* feelings) unavailable to either of the parties operating separately.

Then, too, many conflicts between people are very complex, particularly in organizations where differences arise over complicated technological matters, sensitive financial issues, and sticky human problems. Often these conflicts are resolved much more quickly by involving everyone who possesses relevant data or who might be affected by the decision.

No "Selling" Is Required

You will recall how Method I usually requires that leaders spend time selling their decisions to those who must carry them out, over and above the time involved in simply making the decision. This second step is seldom required in Method III, obviously, because the final decision, once accepted by all the parties to the conflict, needs no selling afterwards—everyone is already sold.

GUIDELINES FOR THE SIX STEPS OF THE NO-LOSE METHOD

As I explained previously, the No-lose Method for resolving conflict between people is just a special application of problem-solving. And effective problem-solving, as you have seen, involves six separate steps. Understanding these six steps and learning what to do to keep the process progressing through each step are the keys to effective problem-solving.

Ideally, before you try the No-lose Method, all persons involved in the conflict should understand the differences between Methods I and II and Method III (the No-lose Method). They should know what the six steps are and why they are critical to effective problem-solving. You may need to remind them that the goal of the No-lose Method is to arrive at a solution *acceptable to everyone,* so nobody feels a loser. Only those people directly involved in the conflict should be included in the problem-solving. And don't start the process unless you and the others have set aside a sizable block of time for it. A blackboard or chart pad is most useful, though not essential; pen and pencil may suffice. It is also important that you not go into the meeting with one fixed, preconceived solution, although obviously you may have any number of alternative solutions in mind. The important thing is that you remain open to other solutions. Finally, of greatest importance is your commitment to the No-lose Method and your unwillingness to revert to Method I or give in with Method II.

While the following guidelines apply for a conflict between you and one other person, they are equally appropriate for conflicts involving several persons. For convenience I will use "O" to stand for the other person.

STEP I. Identifying and Defining the Problem.

This is a critical step in problem-solving. First, your statement of the problem should be expressed in a way that does not communicate blame or judgment. Sending I-messages is always the most effective way for stating a problem.

Secondly, after you have stated your feelings, try to verbalize O's side of the conflict. If you don't know what that is, ask O to state his or her position.

Frequently, it will take a while to get the problem or conflict defined accurately. O may need some time to get feelings out. O may initially get angry or defensive. This is the time to use Active Listening. O must have a chance to ventilate feelings; else he or she will not be ready for the remaining steps.

Don't be in a hurry to get to Step II. Be sure you understand O's point of view, and be sure you state yours accurately and congruently.

Don't understate your own feelings. If you do, O may not feel very motivated to enter into problem-solving.

Frequently, a problem will get redefined as it is discussed—the initial statement of the problem may turn out to be superficial. O's statement of feelings may cause you to see the problem in a new light.

Before moving to Step II, be sure both of you accept the definition of the problem. Test this out—ask if O accepts that this is the problem you both are going to try to solve. Are both sets of needs accurately stated? Don't define the problem as a conflict between competing *solutions*. Define it in terms of conflicting *needs* and then generate your solutions.

Lastly, make certain O understands clearly that you both are looking for a solution that will meet both sets of needs, one that will be acceptable to both—nobody is to lose.

STEP II. Generating Alternate Solutions.

This is the creative part of problem-solving. It is frequently hard to come up with a good solution right away. Initial solutions are seldom adequate, but they may stimulate better ones. Ask O first for possible solutions—you'll have plenty of time to offer yours. At all costs, avoid being evaluative and critical of O's solutions. *Use Active Listening.* Treat O's ideas with respect.

Try to get a number of possible solutions before evaluating or discussing any particular one. Discourage evaluation until a number of possible solutions are proposed. Remember you are trying to generate good solutions, not just any solution.

If things bog down, state the problem again. Sometimes this will start the wheels turning.

Generally, it will become apparent when to move into Step III—after you have come up with a number of reasonably feasible solutions or when one solution appears to be far superior to the others.

STEP III. Evaluating the Alternate Solutions.

This is the stage of problem-solving where you must take special care to be honest; and of course you want O to be honest, too. Both of you will want to do a lot of critical thinking. Are there flaws in any of the possible

solutions? Any reason why a solution might not work? Will
it be too hard to implement or carry out? Is it fair to both?
Use Active Listening.

In evaluating the solutions already generated, one of
you may think of a brand-new one, better than any of the
others. Or you'll hit on a modification that improves an
earlier idea.

If you fail to test solutions at this stage, you'll increase
the chance of ending up with a poor solution, or one that
will not be carried out earnestly.

STEP IV. Decision-making.

A mutual commitment to one solution is essential. Usually when all the facts get exposed, one clearly superior
solution stands out.

Don't make the mistake of trying to persuade or push a
solution on O. If O doesn't freely choose a solution acceptable to him or her, chances are it will not be carried out.

When it appears that perhaps you are close to a decision, state the solution to make certain you both understand what you are about to decide.

STEP V. Implementing the Solution.

It is, of course, one thing to arrive at a creative solution,
another to carry it out. Immediately after a solution has
been agreed upon, it is generally necessary to talk about
implementation.

WHO does WHAT by WHEN?

The most constructive attitude is one of complete trust
that O will faithfully carry out the decision, rather than to
raise the question of what is to be done if O doesn't. So it
is not wise to talk about penalties for failure to implement
a solution at this time.

However, if O fails to carry out his or her end of the
agreement, confront with I-messages. You also may be

able to offer suggestions to help O remember what is to be done.

Don't fall into the trap of constantly reminding O to carry out tasks—O would then grow dependent on your reminders rather than assume full responsibility for his or her own behavior.

Persons unaccustomed to Method III problem-solving in the past may at first be lax in carrying out the solution, especially if they have been used to Method II. Be prepared to do a lot of confronting until they get the idea that you are not going to permit them to "get by." Don't delay too long before confronting them.

STEP VI. *Follow-up Evaluation of the Solution.*

Not all solutions from Method III problem-solving turn out to be the best. Sometimes you or O will discover weaknesses in the solution, in which case the problem should be returned for more problem-solving. Sometimes it is important to ask how O feels now about the solution.

Both of you should have an understanding that decisions are always open for revision, but that neither of you can unilaterally modify a decision. Modifications have to be mutually agreed upon, as was the initial decision.

Sometimes those new to Method III will discover that they overcommitted themselves—in their enthusiasm they agreed to do too much or to do the impossible. Be sure to keep the door open for revision should this happen.

REMEMBER:

Your best tools for effective problem-solving will always be:

Active listening

Clear and honest sending

Respect for the needs of the other

Trust

Being open to new data

Persistence

Firmness in your unwillingness to have it fail

Refusal to revert to Method I or Method II

PROBLEMS IN USING THE NO-LOSE METHOD

Even under the best of conditions leaders will run into problems using the No-lose Method. Seldom does it work without a hitch. At times you'll feel frustrated because it takes more time than you expected. Or you can't find an acceptable solution right away. You'll also run into the situation where someone fails to stick to the agreement. Sometimes you'll be tempted to chuck the whole process and revert to the Method I power approach. On occasion you'll get irritated or angry with your group members when they won't open up and express their feelings; or when they are much too frank in their criticism of your ideas or too stubborn in defending theirs.

Again: it is only realistic for leaders to expect that the No-lose Method involves trade-offs—costs go with the benefits, problems go with the rewards. Each leader must decide whether the benefits are worth the costs. Being aware of some of the problems in the use of the No-lose Method may help you assess whether the benefits are worth the effort.

Do You Want Open and Honest Relationships?

Most leaders would quickly answer that question affirmatively because, at least in the abstract, open and honest relationships with others sounds like a goal most people would consider ideal. Yet open and honest relationships between leaders and group members in most organizations seldom exist. Leaders play the "boss role" and group members play the "subordinate role."

The captain of the ship is supposed to appear as if everything is under control even though there are storms; the boss is supposed to keep up a front of being cool, calm, and collected. Leaders are to give orders and tell people what they should do, leaders should not share their fears or admit their mistakes. Leaders hide their human-ness.

Subordinates are supposed to accept orders and take their boss's advice. They are not to be critical of bosses nor question their judgments. They hide their feelings and cover up their mistakes. Being honest is too dangerous, being assertive too presumptuous.

An engineer in a large midwestern chemical company talked to his L.E.T. instructor about this:

"Most of our foremen are individuals who by dint of being a little smarter, having more pride in their work, and being more aggressive, have become foremen. What that means to them in their culture is that they now are a *boss*, in the full sense of the word 'boss.' And bosses behave in a certain way—like never asking anybody's opinion. Bosses *tell* people, and they're not concerned about anything but getting production. The culture says this is the way you are to behave, and the whole reason for working so hard to become a foreman is so you can be a boss. Some of them are going to say, 'I don't want to share my power.' "

When leaders stop using their power and try to resolve conflicts with the No-lose Method, people drop their roles and their masks. With the growing realization on the part of subordinates that their boss genuinely wants solutions to conflicts that will satisfy their needs, they begin to express those needs openly and honestly. And when subordinates are convinced that conflicts won't result in decisions in which they lose, they stop being afraid of confronting the boss with their real feelings. It works the other way, too. Leaders become more open and honest with subordinates.

Method III introduces into the leader-member relationship a new norm: it is safe to let your hair down and drop your defenses in a conflict situation because eventually a solution will be found that is acceptable to everyone involved.

This means that if you use Method III, you are certain to hear feelings, criticisms, and complaints that are seldom expressed to authoritarian leaders. Are you ready for this? Can you accept hearing how you come across to others? Can you take criticism or having people disagree with your ideas and opinions without defensiveness or retaliation?

When Acceptable Solutions Are Hard to Come By

The question I am most often asked in L.E.T. classes is, "What if you simply can't come up with a mutually acceptable solution?"

I think the main reason this question comes up so often is that people who have little or no experience with Method III are genuinely skeptical about the chances that people in conflict will find no-lose solutions. They haven't seen it happen, so they are sure it won't.

The facts are, it does happen often. But it is also true that sometimes mutually acceptable solutions are hard to find. Stalemates in conflict resolution may develop because the parties did not follow the six steps of the problem-solving process. Or one (or both) of the contestants is still in a win-lose posture and a power-struggle frame of mind. And, needless to say, some conflicts are so complex that it takes a lot of creativity and resourcefulness to come up with good solutions.

Here are methods that have sometimes worked when a mutually acceptable solution is slow in coming:

1. Go back to Step II and try to generate additional alternative solutions.

2. Go back to Step I and try to redefine the problem—there may be an underlying problem that is not being talked about—a "hidden agenda."

3. Make a direct appeal to the people involved, such as, "Can anyone help us understand why we're having trouble finding an acceptable solution? What is impeding us?"

4. See if everyone involved would be willing to "sleep on it" and resume problem-solving later.

5. Ask if more study is needed, more data, additional facts. If so, a task group could be assigned the job and asked to report back to the group. Or maybe a pilot study can be conducted.

6. Perhaps the group would consider calling in an outside consultant.

7. Focus again on the respective *needs* of the parties so as to get away from competing *solutions*.

8. If there are sufficient reasons why a solution must be reached now or very soon, inform the others of these time pressures and the consequences of failing to meet them.

9. See if the group would be willing to try out one of the solutions for a limited period on an experimental basis.

In Chapter X, I will explain how unresolved conflicts or stalemates between a leader and a group member in formal organizations can be handled with the help of the leader's own superior.

While these methods are useful for handling decision stalemates once they occur, in the long run *preventing* stalemates should be the leader's goal. It takes time. Eventually, attitudes of mutual trust and mutual consideration will develop, as people successfully resolve more and more of their conflicts with the No-lose Method. It's true: nothing succeeds like success.

The Leader's Area of Freedom

If you think of No-lose conflict-resolution as a form of delegation of decision-making authority from the leader to all the persons involved in the conflict (including the leader, of course), it becomes obvious that leaders can delegate no more decision-making authority than they actually have.

A supervisor of a group of door-to-door cosmetics saleswomen should never employ the No-lose Method to try to resolve a conflict over how much the saleswomen should charge customers for a particular product, when the retail price of that product has been predetermined by the top management of the company. The issue of product price is clearly *outside the area of freedom of the supervisor.* So is how much gets withheld from monthly paychecks for income tax (a federal law), or how much sales tax is charged the customer (a state law).

Every leader's freedom to make decisions has limits restricting the number of issues that are legitimate for negotiation through problem-solving. Failure to understand this reality is the cause of much misunderstanding about the No-lose Method. For example, some leaders in our L.E.T. classes resist the idea of Method III on the grounds that "leaders can't possibly problem-solve with group members all their differences and disagreements." Of course not. Nor should they try. Many issues will be outside the leader's area of freedom and therefore non-negotiable.

Think of the square below as defining the total hypothetical freedom of a leader (if there were absolutely no limits):

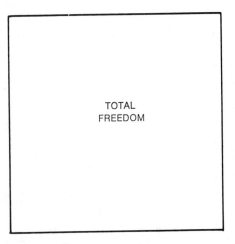

Most leaders' freedom is limited by federal laws—for example, the minimum wage law:

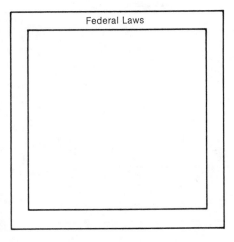

There are limits imposed by state laws—for example, workers must wear protective glasses in the shop:

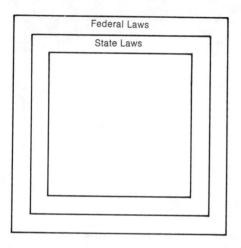

Of course there are company rules such as work hours or number of coffee breaks.

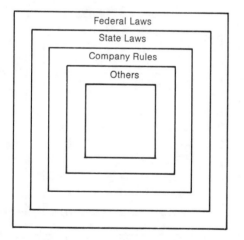

In addition, department heads are subject to policies of their division heads, supervisors are subject to policies of their department heads, and so on.

In actuality, then, most leaders have a relatively small

area of freedom in which to employ the No-lose Method, and the lower down they are in the organizational hierarchy, the smaller their area of freedom.

What can leaders do if conflicts arise in their groups involving issues outside their area of freedom? Here are some suggestions:

1. Tell your group members that the issue is nonnegotiable and why.

2. Active Listen to their complaints so you can understand just how and why their needs are not being met.

3. Invite their ideas as to what might be a better rule.

4. If you agree, you can become a strong advocate for that change within your own organizational family (in your boss's management team).

5. If it gets turned down, go back to your group and tell them why. And be prepared to Active Listen to their feelings.

The last two suggestions contain an important principle. Research has shown that supervisors who are *not* strong and effective advocates (spokesmen) for their group members (in the management group directly above) have workers with lower morale and lower productivity than leaders who *are* strong and effective advocates. This confirms what I have been stressing all along: an *effective* leader is one who is regarded by group members as successful in getting their needs met. So leaders who fail to adequately represent their members to higher levels of management will be perceived as weak leaders, unable to get members what they need.

The Temptation to Revert to Win-lose Methods

Every leader, no matter how committed to the No-lose Method, occasionally will be tempted to fall back on one of the win-lose methods when a mutually acceptable solution to a conflict is slow in coming. It's only natural. Feeling the pressure of a deadline, becoming frustrated and impatient, or getting exasperated with someone who won't come around to their position, leaders sometimes get to the point where they want to say, "All right, damn it, if we can't agree on anything, I'm going to decide what's to be done."

Is there anything wrong with that? After all, it's the leader's responsibility to see that decisions are made, and if all the parties to the conflict won't come up with a mutually acceptable decision, isn't it the leader's duty to step in and make the decision?

Consider the consequences of such action: some group members will be resentful or angry, some will resist carrying out the leader's unilateral decision, and all the group members learn a lesson which they will not soon forget—namely, our leader is capable of reverting to the use of power when things don't go the way he or she would like. This is the lesson learned by a top executive in one of the companies where I was a consultant some years ago:

"In our staff meetings we use the democratic method of making decisions, but only if we come up with a decision the boss likes. When we don't, he makes the decision. Now we feel what's the use of going through all the long discussions to find a solution, he's going to get his way in the end."

Is there any way to avoid such a reaction? One approach I've seen work is for the leader to ask the group if everyone would be willing to have the deadlock broken having him or her make the decision:

"We can't seem to find a solution acceptable to everyone, and we all know some decision has to be made. So would the group accept my making the decision in this case?"

Not infrequently, group members are more than willing, preferring that to prolonged wrangling. If there are strong objections, the leader should back off and resume the problem-solving.

Just as tempting as reverting to Method I is for leaders to give in to a decision unacceptable to them (Method II). This, too, has severe consequences. In the first place, the leader will likely feel resentful afterwards. Secondly, this act of permissiveness teaches the group members a lesson, too—namely, if we hold off long enough for what we want, our leader will eventually give in.

Consensus, Majority, and Mutual Acceptance

Much misunderstanding about (and resistance to) the No-lose Method derives from the failure of most people to comprehend the precise meanings of three words: "consensus," "majority," and "mutual acceptance." All three terms represent possible criteria for determining what decision a group shall make.

While the term consensus is commonly used to mean *complete* or *unanimous* agreement, its precise (dictionary) meaning is *general* agreement. A second definition is "majority of opinion." However, when people say, "We make decisions by consensus," they usually mean that everyone agrees, not just a majority of those voting (agreement "in general").

Majority is commonly understood as "the number larger than half the total, as opposed to the minority" (though for certain decisions some groups require a "two-thirds majority").

Consensus, obviously, is less precise than majority because "general agreement" fails to indicate exactly how many agree and how many disagree. Majority, however, specifies that at least half, and maybe more, agree. Now, when a group arrives at a particular decision by a majority voting approval, the majority wins and the minority loses —a win-lose outcome. The almost universal criterion for decision-making in most groups is "majority rule," a euphemism for majority wins, minority loses. This does not sound like the No-lose Method of decision-making, and it is not.

Then how does a No-lose decision get made? Not by taking a vote, at least not in the sense that the term vote is generally used. This is why I emphasize that the No-lose Method never calls for a vote; in fact, voting is antithetical to No-lose decision-making. A No-lose decision is made only when it becomes apparent that all the members of the group, *including the leader,* are willing to *accept* that decision—what I call "mutual acceptance." Note that I did not say that the members all *agree* with the decision because sometimes people are willing to accept a solution yet not be in agreement with it—or at least not in complete agreement with it.

This still leaves the question of how one determines when all group members have reached the point of mutual acceptance of a decision. This can be accomplished in several ways:

1. The leader may ask, "Does everyone accept this decision?" If everyone nods or says "yes," the decision is considered final.

2. The leader may ask, "Is anyone opposed to this decision?" If no one speaks, it is assumed everyone accepts the decision.

3. Any *group member* may do either 1 or 2 above.

These methods may be a form of voting, although I much prefer to describe this essential closing function the way the Quakers do: "getting the sense of the meeting." It is much like taking a straw vote, not to determine final results but to find out if everyone is ready to accept a decision. If someone is not ready—and this includes the leader, of course—the problem-solving is not finished.

When people say, "After all, the leader is still leader, and will be held accountable for all decisions, so he can't go along with all group decisions," they do not understand that in the No-lose Method there is no *group* decision until *everyone* accepts the decision, including the leader. And, as I have repeatedly emphasized, because leaders are held accountable for decisions made by their group, they would be fools to go along with a decision they cannot accept.

Does the Group Have to Decide Everything?

This question reflects another misunderstanding about the No-lose Method. It is based on a legitimate concern that, if group decision-making is required for *every* problem, it would take so much time that "no work would ever get done." In reality, a very large percent of decisions are made in organizations without any group participation. And they should be. Here is how I feel about my own job:

In the course of a day in my role as president of an organization I make many decisions: I decide to accept an invitation to speak to a group in Indianapolis; I turn down another invitation; I decide to postpone a meeting I had previously set up; I agree to have an appointment with a colleague who wants to find out what our organization is doing; I make a decision that one of our courses needs revision and updating; I decide that all departments must reduce costs at least 10 percent for the remainder of the year; I decide to seek a short-term loan from the bank; I decide we need a new policy for offering our courses in Sweden; I decide to write a letter of thanks to one of our instructors in Canada.

Obviously, I felt it necessary to make all of these decisions to carry out the "responsibilities of my office," my duties as spelled out in my job description, the requirements of my job. Recall the discussion in Chapter VIII of Authority $_J$, the sanctioned authority of one's job. By virtue of the authority vested in my position, I make hundreds of decisions.

It is another matter when I encounter conflicts in my relations with others, conflicts over issues that will seriously affect others or conflicts about what decision should be made to solve a problem I have taken to my management team. These conflicts I choose to resolve with the No-lose Method rather than risk the negative consequences of using my power with Method I.

There are other decisions that are not made by the group. Frequently in the course of problem-solving, a group delegates decision-making responsibility to the leader or a group member or a task force.

A management team begins to deal with a problem on its agenda—i.e., the adequacy of the company's medical and hospitalization plan. After several minutes of defining the problem, the group delegates full responsibility to the business manager for investigating different plans offered by several other insurance carriers, after which he is assigned the authority to choose the best. He accepts the assignment, and in the next few weeks he alone completes Steps II–V of the problem-solving process: exploring alternative plans, evaluating each, making a final decision and implementing it.

The wisdom of groups can be trusted, much more often than we think. Group members don't want to decide everything—just what they judge to be most crucial to getting their needs met and meeting the needs of the organization, in which, of course, they too have an important stake. With many other issues, they usually prefer having someone else take on the often laborious task of problem-solving.

When Agreements Are Not Honored

While Method III generates much stronger motivation for people to carry out the ultimate decision than does Method I, all leaders should be prepared to handle cases of one or more group members failing to honor the decision. Contemplating this, leaders often ask, "Isn't Method I (or power) necessary and justified when people don't stick to their agreements or carry out their part of the bargain?" Again, the temptation to punish, warn, threaten, or reprimand in this situation has its origins in people's past experiences, particularly during childhood, when those were the very reactions of adults to the child's failure to honor agreements.

The use of power to enforce compliance or to punish noncompliance to a No-lose decision will bring on the same consequences (coping mechanisms and damaged relationships) as using power in making the decision. Alternative nonpower methods will be less risky and usually more effective:

1. Try a reminder: verbally or with a memo.

2. Use I-messages for, after all, a person's not honoring an agreement is certainly unacceptable to you.

3. Bring the issue of noncompliance back to the group for problem-solving: "We made a decision, but it has come to my attention that some of us have not carried it out. How can we deal with this?"

Deciding Who Should Be Included In The Problem-Solving

Leaders sometimes involve more people than necessary in a problem-solving session, or they exclude people who should be involved. Too many people in a meeting can impede the problem-solving process; and if some people have no interest in the problem they resent the encroachment on their productive work time. Being excluded from a problem-solving session can also produce resentment, especially if the person has a stake in how the problem gets resolved. People also can interpret exclusion as evidence that they are not valued in the organization—it can be a blow to their self-esteem.

While no system can fit every situation, deciding who to include in each problem-solving session can be easier for leaders if they understand one very important principle about decisions.

Usually people think about decisions only in terms of *quality*. "Is this decision good or bad?" "Did we end up making a high- or a low-quality decision?" While the quality of a decision is an important criterion against which to judge it, it is not the only criterion. A top executive with whom I worked when consulting with his organization somewhat jokingly made this admission:

"In the past I prided myself on making high-quality decisions, and I made a lot of damned good decisions. The only problem was they weren't always accepted by the people who had to carry them out."

Decisions must be evaluated on their quality, yes, but also on the degree of *acceptance* from the people who have to implement them.

This commonsense principle can help leaders decide whom to invite to a problem-solving session. When you are faced with this problem, you need to ask yourself two questions:

Who has the relevant data?

Who will be affected by the decision?

The first question reflects your concern about the *quality* of the ultimate decision, the second your desire that the decision receive maximum *acceptance*. Bringing in the people who have relevant data obviously increases your chances of getting a high-quality decision. But why include people who will be affected by the decision? Remember the "principle of participation" I described earlier: when people have a voice in making a decision they will have more motivation to implement it.

A supervisor in a large St. Louis manufacturing plant obviously recognized the importance of the Principle of Participation and had his own explanation of why it works:

"Take a simple thing, like gloves for the workers. The ones we bought them they never did like. They were 'women's gloves,' 'too stiff,' 'too hard.' So we flew in several samples out of Chicago and let them pick the ones they wanted. They didn't agree a hundred percent on them but when it came down to the most votes for one pair, that's what they got. And now they're not saying nothing about them right now. I think that if you are part of suggesting a decision, if you then turn around and say it's no good, it's like saying, 'I'm stupid.' You can't stand there and act like the decision was all the foreman's fault—or the company's —when you have had something to do with picking the decision. The other guys would notice it if you did."

There Is No Turning Back

Over the years I have become convinced that a commitment to use the No-lose Method for resolving conflicts all but eliminates a leader's option of going back to the authoritarian method. Give people the experience of what it's like to resolve conflicts so that nobody loses, and they will strongly resist having it taken away. Perhaps it's like a "point of no return"—once group members get accustomed to having a leader who is respectful of their needs, they will not tolerate a return to a previous condition of lesser need satisfaction.

Perhaps we have stumbled onto a new principle in human relationships, one that leaders would do well to understand before undertaking a change toward using the No-lose Method. Why this principle operates can be explained in a number of ways.

First, what initially seems like a gift or privilege, as the No-lose Method is usually first perceived when people are unaccustomed to such treatment, in time becomes felt as a *right*. And then people will fight any attempts to have that right denied them, just as surely as those groups in our country who, after finally gaining the franchise, would now fight any attempt to have it taken away.

Secondly, leaders who begin to employ Method III in effect are *educating* their group members, showing by their behavior a totally new and different way of resolving conflicts. Once group members understand how different Method III is, they will easily recognize Method I, should the leader revert back to using it again. And don't think they won't call the leader's attention to it!

We first discovered this in families in which the children had become accustomed to their parents using the No-lose Method. If ever one of the parents slipped back to using coercive power, their kids would call them on it.

Some years ago in my own family, my daughter, then around 11 years old, and I got into a conflict about her eating habits. I was objecting to her eating so much sugar and carbohydrate and so little protein and vegetables. I came on much too strong with my power: "Well, we simply won't have desserts any more" and "No sweet stuff for your afterschool snacks." Looking up from my plate I saw my daughter holding up her right hand with only her index finger extended. As I looked, she whispered audibly, "Method I!" Believe me, I dropped my power posture forthwith.

Organizational leaders, too, will find that once their subordinates get used to a climate where conflicts are never handled coercively, any deviation may produce unusually strong negative reactions. Understandably, even one use of power will stand out like a sore thumb. Subordinates will be shocked and angry, not unlike the strong reactions of most people to President Nixon's behavior, which deviated so far from the norms of ethical behavior that everyone had come to expect from the President of our country.

You will recall my earlier assertion: *the existence of a leader's power is made visible only through its use.* Unfortunately, the trust and security a leader may build up from years of refusing to use power may be severely diminished by one momentary act of using power, much as the faith and trust built up in a marriage by years of fidelity can be shattered by one act of infidelity on the part of one's spouse.

Does this mean that leaders who decide to give up power must be paragons who never fail to practice what they preach and never take a step backward? Not at all. In the first place, once you decide to use the No-lose Method, you'll get constant help from your group members in the form of reminders if ever you start to slip back to power methods. This feedback definitely will help you learn to practice what you preach. Secondly, if on occasion you happen to revert to hauling out your power, there are constructive actions you can take afterwards:

1. Explain to the group why you took unilateral action. There may be logical reasons they'll understand—e.g., time pressure, you were harassed and upset, previous Method III attempts had failed, danger was clear and present, etc.

2. Use Active Listening to demonstrate your understanding and acceptance of their negative feelings.

3. Initiate problem-solving to prevent similar situations from arising in the future.

4. Apologize, but only if you genuinely feel like it, of course.

While I have pointed out the pitfalls of "turning back" once you have made the commitment to the No-lose Method, it is equally important to emphasize another principle: when your people get convinced that you are really sincere about trying to solve conflicts with the No-lose Method, they'll do things to help you reach that goal and they'll be more understanding than you think if you trip once in a while along the way. Nevertheless, the use of power often causes resentment, hostility, and retaliation. And, as everyone knows, people have a tendency to reject the influence of someone toward whom they have strong negative feelings. Patients who hate their doctor have a tendency to resist his or her advice or counsel. Students who grow to hate a teacher won't allow themselves to learn from that teacher, no matter how much knowledge he or she might possess. Children are seldom influenced by the experience and wisdom of parents whose use of power has made the kids dislike or hate them.

Yet most people are convinced they need power to increase their influence over others. They quickly forget their own firsthand experience with people who used power over them, which should convince leaders that the more they use power, the less influence they will have (another high cost of Method I and the coercion it requires).

X. ORGANIZATIONAL APPLICATIONS OF THE NO-LOSE METHOD

WHILE I have so far illustrated the No-lose Method primarily with conflicts between a leader and a single group member, the nonpower way of resolving conflicts works in many other situations. In fact, leaders who become competent in using Method III find that it becomes a "way of life," an integral part of *all* their organizational relationships. Leaders who replace their former win-lose approach with the No-lose Method find themselves automatically, and perhaps unconsciously, approaching all conflict situations with a "we" attitude, as opposed to an "I" attitude:

We have a problem	vs.	I have a problem with this person
We need to get together	vs.	I need to think this out
We must find a solution	vs.	I must find a solution

This "relationship thinking" carries over into all conflict situations: between the leader and other leaders at the same level in the organizational structure, between the leader and all group members, between the leader and union representatives, between the leader and his or her supervisor, or between members of a task force. In those organizations where I first trained all members of the top management team in the use of the No-lose Method, I watched this new thinking permeate downward and throughout the entire organization, making "mutual need satisfaction" the norm for every leader, in all relationships.

CONFLICTS BETWEEN LEADERS AND ALL GROUP MEMBERS

As would be expected, at some time leaders will come into conflict with all of their people. It may not happen often, but it does happen, particularly when all group members somehow fall into a pattern of doing something in concert that the boss finds unacceptable, as in the case of the scooter problem described by a graduate of L.E.T., who was a plant manager of a large manufacturing company spread out over several acres:

"The Method III I've used a number of times, and it's been real effective. We have electric scooters in the shop and each foreman is assigned a scooter. They can go from the farthest corner of the plant to the farthest corner in three minutes. Right after I came to work I'd get bugged when I saw the mechanics all riding the foremen's scooters—all they do is tear them up and when the foremen need them they don't have them. One day I had to wait ten minutes after I called a foreman and he said he'd be right down. I saw his scooter being ridden by a mechanic—big old pipe wrenches hanging out the back, and here he comes late, walking around the corner. That's when I decided to use Method III. I got all of my staff together, put my problem up on the blackboard, put a bunch of my needs down, and had them put their needs down. And when we got all done, they were really shook up about the mechanics using their scooters and they decided to keep their own scooters and not let the mechanics ride them. That's been over a year ago. And I haven't had a bit of a problem since. I found out they wanted to keep good relations with their mechanics and didn't want to tell their best buddy, 'You can't use my scooter.' But I bent just a little. I agreed that if the guy's going to be back in a couple of minutes, fine, let him use it. But not to take your scooter and go out and troubleshoot for a long time or go from building to building."

Only the plant manager regarded scooters as a problem, so it was up to him to take the initiative to get his staff together, confront them with his concerns, and start the problem-solving process. What surfaced, in this case, was that the foremen were torn between their need to be "good guys" in the eyes of the mechanics and their need to have scooters always available for use. A mutually acceptable solution was reached—in this case, a compromise of sorts.

COMPANY-UNION CONFLICTS

Conflicts between "management" and unions have been with us since unions came into being. Strangely, there isn't much information about the methods of conflict resolution most frequently employed in these common conflicts. Despite the terms typically used to describe their procedures—"negotiations," "bargaining"—I suspect that both management and labor approach conflicts predominantly with a win-lose posture. In fact, bargaining generally implies that each of the parties to a conflict goes in with a preconceived "bargaining position" from which to begin negotiations. I do remember reading about one successful conflict-resolution effort that sounded very much like our No-lose Method: when the International Ladies Garment Workers Union and garment industry owners, during the Depression, agreed to institute a blanket reduction in the workers' wages rather than face massive layoffs or company shutdowns.

I find no evidence that the No-lose Method is widely used in labor-management negotiations. Too often this relationship is a continuous power struggle; solutions to serious conflicts appear to have a *lose-lose* quality—neither party getting what they really want. Nevertheless, it is encouraging that in a few cases L.E.T. graduates have used the No-lose Method in management-union conflicts. Here is one involving a conflict over work schedules, submitted by an industrial relations executive:

"The company was interested in getting more flexibility in the way we schedule, but the union contract for at least twenty years prevented us from adopting this kind of scheduling. They just wouldn't hear of it. Well, we set up a joint subcommittee and we decided to use the L.E.T. approach—Method III problem-solving. We told them we had certain needs and that we knew they had needs and what we wanted to do was talk about what those needs were. We listed all the needs the company had and explained the best we could why those needs were what they were. We told them we wanted to know what their needs were, too. We wound up with a list of thirty-five areas where we had needs. Some of them turned out to be joint needs. We then went back over them and decided which ones would be recategorized, which would require negotiation, and which would be changed by new policies. Others we found out weren't serious problems at all, once we used the brainstorming method. Some of them we threw out. At any rate, we used that method all the way through and came up with a list of seven specific recommendations for things that had to be done that were acceptable to the union committee members. . . . And I think it succeeded beyond our dreams. . . . It was basically a Method III problem-solving situation. There were occasions when we were unsuccessful in keeping them on the agenda and when that happened we tried to use the Active Listening. For the list of our thirty-five problems, we developed solutions for perhaps twenty to twenty-three of them. The others were either thrown out or we decided there wasn't anything we could do about them. . . . And they seemed very happy with that."

The possibilities for employing the No-lose Method in such union-management negotiations seem very promising, but it would require a change in attitude on the part of both parties away from a win-lose and toward a no-lose stance. In the future we will certainly see much wider acceptance of employee participation in key management decisions in industrial organizations. In Sweden and Germany, for example, such joint participation, or "codetermination," has recently been mandated by law. The law requires that employees must be represented on the board of directors of all business and industrial organizations, giving them a voice in all decisions that might affect employees. Obviously, where codetermination is practiced, the No-lose Method would appear to be vastly superior to win-lose methods.

HANDLING COMPLAINTS FROM LOWER LEVELS

A common problem for all leaders is what to do when a member of one of your subordinate's groups comes to you with a complaint arising from some unmet need. Typically, when a person makes such an appeal to his boss's boss, it is called "going over your boss's head." This is almost universally condemned as reprehensible. Discussions about this problem in our L.E.T. classes always produce the strongest of feelings from participants:

"That's insubordination!"

"It should be strongly discouraged."

"Going over your boss's head is inviting trouble."

"I'd fire the son of a bitch that went over my head."

Obviously, leaders have a lot of fear and anxiety about this situation. Yet it does happen, sometimes frequently. Usually being afraid of a situation means that you don't know how to handle it effectively. This is true of most leaders, and the reason is not hard to find: they see "going over the boss's head" in win-lose terms. When a person comes to a leader, bypassing his or her boss (the leader's subordinate), that leader feels caught in a dilemma—whose side shall he take, who is going to win? No leader wants a disgruntled or unhappy employee; neither does he want to alienate a subordinate (the employee's boss). The most common way out is to decide in favor of the employee's supervisor, according to the familiar (but misguided) principle of "A leader should always back up his people in conflicts with their employees," or "Don't ever undermine the authority of one of your subordinates."

A much more satisfactory way is readily available to leaders, if they would only shift into the no-lose way of thinking about conflicts. Here is how the No-lose Method would work in such a situation:

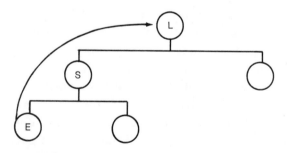

As represented by the arrow, E (a male employee) has bypassed S (a male supervisor) and come to L (the leader, a woman) with a complaint. Here are the steps L can follow:

1. L must listen empathically and understandingly, not, however, to discover what the problem is, but to demonstrate her acceptance (not agreement) of E's feelings and perhaps help E find his own solution.

2. If E finds a solution that meets his needs, the problem is solved.

3. If E does not, L asks E to consider going directly to S with the complaint, instructing E to send only I-messages to S.

4. If E is willing to go directly to S, L is now out of the problem.

5. If E is reluctant to go directly to S, L offers E the alternative of calling S to come join them to work out a solution acceptable to both E and S (Method III).

6. If E rejects this alternative, L explains her unwillingness to make any decisions in the absence of S.

7. If E accepts having S join them, L asks S to come in, explaining briefly that L has learned of a problem that involves S and E and would like to help, but both must be present.

8. L then acts only as a neutral facilitator of problem-solving between S and E, staying completely out of the specific content of the problem, yet Active Listening and helping S and E work through the six steps of the problem-solving process and reach some solution mutually acceptable to both S and E.

While this procedure may look rather detailed or mechanical, every step has a purpose. The leader first wants to show acceptance and understanding of the employee so that in the future he won't be discouraged from trying to get his needs met. The leader must communicate that the employee owns the problem, yet be willing to help him find a solution on his own, if possible. The leader also must communicate that she is unable to help without both parties present. Finally, the leader must not get drawn into problem-solving.

This procedure produces some tangible and long-range benefits to all parties:

1. The employee learns that the leader will not referee conflicts between him and his supervisor.

2. The employee learns it is expected that he first try to resolve conflicts with his supervisor by going directly to him.

3. The supervisor learns that the leader will not interfere in conflicts with his employees by making unilateral decisions in his absence. Equally important, the leader will not brush off an employee complaint by automatically "backing up the supervisor."

4. Both employee and supervisor learn that the leader values conflicts getting resolved by mutual problem-solving rather than by some universal rule that a supervisor is always right because he's the boss (or the opposite: an employee's needs must be met at any cost).

5. The supervisor learns from this that it would also be acceptable for him to go over the leader's head should he have an unresolved conflict with the leader.

WHEN YOUR NEEDS ARE FRUSTRATED BY YOUR BOSS

Leaders, no less than group members, find themselves unable to get their needs met because of some action by their superior. Without consulting you, your boss makes a decision that interferes with your doing your best job or deprives you of something you need. Now what do you do? Or your boss settles a conflict between the two of you by using Method I, causing you to feel he won, you lost. Must that be the end of it? Must you be resolved to grin and bear it? Unfortunately, many leaders do grin and bear it, although their grin is usually a cover-up for resentment and anger.

Yet, doing nothing when your superior has made a decision unfavorable and unacceptable to you is sanctioned and supported by commonly accepted "principles of management," such as

"An order is an order."

"Subordinates' first responsibility is to follow orders, no matter how much they disagree with them."

"Never go over your superior's head."

"Managers can never make a decision acceptable to everyone."

An opposing point of view, more compatible with our concept of organizational effectiveness, is that when decisions deprive people of their needs they should be questioned or challenged. People sometimes make bad decisions without knowing what the consequences will be. The critical question is: how can a person go about getting a decision modified without hurting the relationship with his or her superior?

Again, the No-lose Method is the key. And there is a definite procedure to follow:

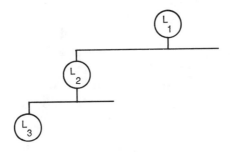

The above diagram shows three levels of leaders (say, all women) in an organization. L_2, a department head, made

a decision that turned out to be unacceptable to L_3, a supervisor, because it made her job much more difficult. Using the No-lose way, L_3 takes the following action:

1. L_3 asks L_2 for a conference at her convenience, briefly explaining the problem.

2. L_3 starts out by sending appropriate I-messages, making sure to shift gears to Active Listening when required. L_3 invites L_2 to join in Method III problem-solving.

3. If L_2 refuses or if Method III fails, L_3 asks L_2 to accompany her in a conference with L_1 with the hope that L_1 might help them find a no-lose solution.

4. If L_2 refuses, L_3 informs L_2 that she intends to go to L_1 for help, but she would much prefer L_2 join her so L_2 can adequately represent her own position to L_1.

5. If L_2 still refuses to join L_3, L_3 goes to L_1, making certain she explains to L_1 that she has already tried Steps 1, 2, 3, and 4.

Under certain circumstances, L_3 might change her mind at any of the above steps and decide to accept L_2's decision. In other words, L_3 would carry out all five steps only if she continues to feel strongly that L_2's decision is unacceptable. Now, when L_1 hears L_3's problem, she should follow the steps outlined previously under Handling Complaints from Lower Levels.

Strangely, we meet strong resistance to this procedure in our L.E.T. classes. Many leaders are afraid to carry out this procedure—it looks much too dangerous to them. They say, "L_2 would fire L_3" or "L_3 would ruin her relationship with L_2."

These leaders are remembering past experiences in organizations and conflicts that were typically resolved by those with the most power, which usually produces win-lose outcomes. It seems foreign to them that conflicts should be resolved by problem-solving designed to produce mutually acceptable solutions.

When leaders *at all levels* are committed to using the

No-lose Method, the above procedure is certainly not odd. Nor is it dangerous. It is perfectly consistent with our model of nonpower, no-lose, problem-solving leadership.

PROBLEM-SOLVING WITH LARGER GROUPS

I have said nothing yet about using no-lose problem-solving when conflicts involve people far removed from the leader's own work group or team. Often in these situations larger numbers of people are involved, and as everyone knows, problem-solving with groups larger than 15 to 20 people can be very difficult. Since social scientists have not yet devised many practical models for participatory problem-solving with large groups, most leaders throw in the towel and end up using Method I.

Yet many problems arise when large numbers of people have relevant data or else will be affected by the ultimate decision, such as:

Should the organization move to another city? If so, how to manage it?

Should salaries and wages be cut or should many employees be laid off during a recession?

Should flexible scheduling for employees to ease the rush-hour problem be adopted?

How can a company-wide reduction of costs be effected?

How is the most cost-effective group medical plan to be found?

Such problems often involve persons at several different levels, from several different departments or divisions, or in some cases all employees or members of the organization. Involving so many people in problem-solving may require (1) breaking the group into smaller groups, (2) having groups choose representatives, or (3) employing a sampling method.

In my work as consultant, I have often been called on

to help companies solve problems requiring the participation of large numbers of people. These challenges forced me to develop two procedures. One I have called the "Down-Up-Down-Up" Method, the other the Evaluation Committee Method. Both were effective in getting the problem solved with maximum participation.

THE "DOWN-UP-DOWN-UP" METHOD

This method evolved in a well-known Los Angeles company where I was consulting at the time. The personnel director shared this problem: there was widespread dissatisfaction with the company's group medical plan. The personnel director was well on his way toward going through the problem-solving process all by himself and was almost to the point of choosing another insurance carrier.

I first sold him on the "participation principle" and eventually got him to employ the following method:

Step 1 (DOWN the organization): This involved taking the problem down through the several levels of the organization via the line supervisors. First, all the divisional vice-presidents were asked to conduct a meeting with all of their department heads. At each meeting the problem was shared and the subordinates were asked for their ideas. Then the department heads conducted similar meetings with their supervisors. Finally, all supervisors conducted similar meetings with their subordinates.

Step 2 (UP the organization): Next, all of the ideas generated in the small groups were submitted to the executive staff (the president and his vice-presidents, plus the personnel director).

Step 3 (DOWN the organization): The executive staff delegated to a task group (the personnel director and one of the vice-presidents) the job of evaluating all of the ideas and then finding a new insurance carrier who would design a health plan that would incorporate the employees' ideas. The plan worked out by the task group (including the insurance carrier representative) was then sent down the line organization via similar meetings to those held in Step 1. The groups were asked to evaluate the plan (Step III in the problem-solving process) and make a decision to accept it, accept it with modifications, or reject it (Step IV in the problem-solving process).

Step 4 (UP the organization): The decisions of each of the groups were then sent up the line organization to the executive staff, which then made final modifications and eventually adopted the amended plan.

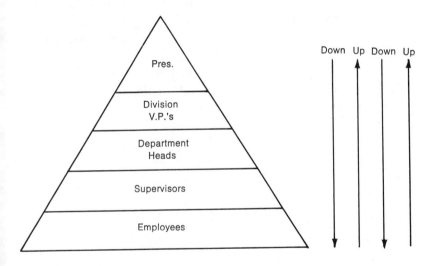

Results

A health plan highly satisfactory to most employees, unique enough to fit the special needs of this company, and far superior to the previous plan.

Good feelings on the part of all levels in the company for having been given the chance to participate in the problem-solving.

Elimination of almost all complaints about the company's health plan.

THE "EVALUATION COMMITTEE" METHOD

This method, too, evolved in a Los Angeles company where I was consulting. I was asked by the president of the company to spend time with the vice-president in charge of the sales division because the vice-president was very concerned about high turnover, low production, and poor morale of the sales force (120 salesmen).

Step 1: I first had to sell the vice-president on the "principle of participation"—involving all the various levels of the sales division in generating solutions to the problem. A method then was designed by me and accepted by the vice-president.

The method for generating solutions (Step II in the problem-solving process) involved my conducting a number of small-group brainstorming meetings with all members of the sales division:

MEETING A: Included the vice-president, the sales trainer, and the three division managers.

MEETING B: All the district managers.

MEETING C:
MEETING D:
MEETING E:
MEETING F: } Each contained around 20 field salesmen.
MEETING G:
MEETING H:

Each brainstorming meeting lasted from 45 to 90 minutes. At the start of each meeting I stated the problem exactly as defined by the vice-president: "The vice-president of sales is very concerned about the problem of high turnover, low productivity, and poor morale in the sales force. I have been asked to conduct a series of meetings like this in order to get everybody's constructive ideas for solving this problem."

Then I spelled out the standard ground rules for brainstorming. Each idea submitted was written on a three-by-five card, then read back to the person who submitted the idea to verify its accuracy.

Step 2: Approximately 150 different solutions were generated in the eight meetings. These were shown to the vice-president, who immediately started through the pile, evaluating each idea—discarding some as "ridiculous," others as "been tried before," others as "cost too much," etc. Fearing a breakdown in the problem-solving, I suggested a second method: select representatives from each group to serve on an "evaluation committee." The task of this committee would be to engage in Steps III and IV of the problem-solving process.

Convincing the vice-president to accept this took several hours of listening plus some support from the president of the company. The vice-president's objections were as follows:

Groups cannot make decisions.

They won't have all the facts.

Salesmen simply are not sufficiently well informed.

It will take too much time.

Lines of authority will be bypassed.

He and the division managers could do the job alone.

Finally, the vice-president was able to accept the evaluation committee method as well as the validity of the principle of participation. My next challenge was selling the idea that the evaluation committee should be allowed to make *final* decisions (Step IV in the problem-solving process) and to function without a chairman (be a leader-less group). Eventually the vice-president agreed to both of these suggestions.

Step 3: The members of the evaluation committee were chosen (those indicated by checks on the chart below). The choices were made to assure representation from all levels, including the sales force (two members). A strategically sound decision was the inclusion of the vice-president on the evaluation committee so that the highest level of authority in the division would be represented, which permitted the evaluation committee to make final decisions.

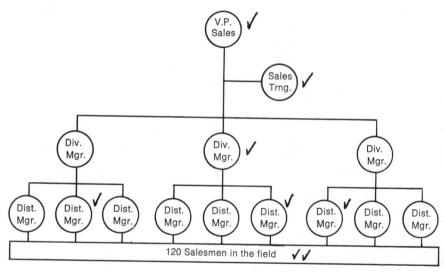

Step 4: The evaluation committee met approximately six times, each session lasting around two hours. They evaluated all the 150 solutions and made decisions on each one. These decisions were:

(1) To implement a solution.

(2) To reject a solution.

(3) To study a solution further and bring in a recommendation to the committee.

Step 5: The committee members decided to feed back to the groups they represented the reasons why certain solutions were rejected. This was done in brief meetings with the sales managers and the salesmen where a committee member explained why the committee took the action it did.

The evaluation committee made major decisions, not merely superficial ones. They grappled with very complicated problems and came out with significant and often very creative decisions, covering such subjects as:

New methods for recruiting prospective salesmen.

New methods for "selection evaluation" at time of hiring.

New methods for improving salesmen training.

A new compensation system for salesmen.

New pricing for various products.

The establishment of a new job—field trainer.

The improvement of the sales "presentation kit" used by salesmen.

Results

Morale increased amazingly.

Production increased.

Turnover decreased.

The time it took to train a new salesman and get him or her into production decreased from five weeks to ten days.

One sales manager said, "We've made more improvements in one month than in the previous five years."

The division decided to institutionalize the entire method and repeat it every year.

WHEN RULES ARE BROKEN

Every organization has rules, and leaders at every level are held accountable for making certain that their people follow them. Some of these rules were in effect long before group members joined the organization; some may have been set by higher authority and hence lie outside "the area of freedom" of leaders at lower levels. Many such rules, obviously, get established without the participation of the people who are expected to abide by them.

What is a leader to do when a member of his or her work group breaks one of these rules? Is there a way to handle such infractions and still operate within the no-lose philosophy?

Here, in outline form, is a step-by-step procedure we teach in the L.E.T. course. Suppose one of your subordinates, Randy, has broken a rule:

1. If you are certain Randy has broken the rule, first determine if he is aware of the rule and understands it. If he does not, explain the rule and your responsibility to enforce it.

2. If Randy, for whatever reason, doesn't feel he can abide by the rule, listen empathically, but explain that you do not have the authority to give him that freedom—it is outside your area of freedom or sphere of influence.

3. If, later, Randy again breaks the rule, you must decide where to locate his rule-breaking behavior within your behavioral rectangle: in your area of Acceptable Behavior (no tangible effect on you) or in your area of Unacceptable Behavior (tangible effect on you).

4. If Randy's breaking the rule is genuinely acceptable to you, you decide to take no action and let him suffer the consequences (he "owns" the problem). Example: if a subordinate parks his car in a space reserved for another, you may decide it doesn't affect you and choose to do nothing.

5. If Randy's behavior is *unacceptable* to you (you "own" the problem), send a very clear I-message. Example—a subordinate fails to

lock up classified materials: "Randy, when classified materials are not locked up, I get very anxious because my boss will hold me accountable and my job might be at stake." You may need to shift gears and Active Listen to his reaction.

6. If Randy still does not change his behavior, you recognize a conflict of needs and initiate Method III. Now you may find out what needs are causing him to break the rule.

7. If Method III does not produce a solution acceptable to you, you can choose one of these alternatives:
(a) Tell him exactly what the consequences will be the next time (whatever they happen to be—fine, dismissal, demotion, etc.).
(b) Administer the consequences this time.
(c) Decide the rule is one that should be changed and take steps to bring the issue up with your superior.

A number of assumptions underlie this approach: people often don't know about rules they break; breaking a rule occurs because people are trying to meet some need; people usually will respond to appeals for them to be considerate of your needs; people must accept the consequences of their behavior if they choose to continue breaking a rule. All these assumptions, as well as the procedure I have outlined, seem consistent with my concept of leader effectiveness.

XI. THE PERIODIC PLANNING CONFERENCE: A NEW APPROACH TO PERFORMANCE EVALUATION

O NE conclusion *consistently* appears in the writings of social scientists who have evaluated the thousands of research studies on leadership in formal organizations. In my own words, it is:

High-productivity groups (high-achievement work groups) have leaders who are successful in fostering and maintaining in their subordinates enthusiasm and motivation for reaching productivity goals which the organization considers necessary to meet its needs.

As their organization's representatives, effective leaders must perform functions that will result in a level of productivity that feels fair or equitable to top management, but not unfair or inequitable to the group members. Whatever these leader functions (behaviors) are—and this is a critical point—they are quite different from "human relations" functions or "person-centered behaviors" that make subordinates feel good: empathic listening, sending nonblaming I-messages, encouraging participation in decision-making, reducing status differentials, fostering group cohesion, showing consideration for subordinates' needs, being nonpunitive, and so on.

So treating people decently, seeing that their needs are met, and removing sources of dissatisfaction *will not* in themselves suffice to bring about high productivity and high achievement. Something else is needed—what in Chapter II I called the "skills to meet the organization's needs." Effective leaders are "task specialists" as well as "human relations" specialists.

High-achievement groups have leaders who somehow get across to group members the expectations of the organization about the needed level of productivity. The *manner* in which leaders develop and communicate their productivity expectations will determine whether they are accepted by the work group.

Here is where human relations skills play such a critical part. If productivity goals are developed unilaterally by the leader with no chance for group participation, or if the leader doesn't listen to their feelings or ideas, or if the leader is punitive when group members have difficulty meeting productivity goals—workers are likely to feel an imbalance exists in the cost/benefit ratio and that they are being exploited in an inequitable relationship. On the other hand, if group members are convinced that the organization is genuinely concerned about their needs and treats people with respect, they are less likely to believe that the organization would make unfair demands on them.

In addition to this feeling of *trust*, group members also need reliable, accurate performance evaluations and the assurance that their performance will be rewarded by tangible benefits. This is why leaders need an effective system for evaluating work performance in their efforts to meet the productivity goals of the organization.

Is the work group accomplishing the goals for which the

leader is accountable? How effectively is each individual performing his or her job? To what extent are the leader's needs being met by the performance of the group and by individual members?

Performance evaluation is not only difficult, but leaders usually dread it because it so often causes conflict between the leader and the group members. Subordinates often resent external evaluation, feel threatened by it, or become argumentative and contentious when they feel the evaluation is unfair, which they usually do.

What improvements can be made? How can performance evaluation take place in a way consistent with the philosophy and theory underlying L.E.T.? What is the best performance evaluation method for a leader who is committed to "management by *mutual* need satisfaction"?

In this chapter I will point out the usual deficiencies of evaluating performance and describe a procedure, the Periodic Planning Conference, which enables leaders to do the job far more effectively and at the same time strengthen relationships and help subordinates grow.

TRADITIONAL PERFORMANCE EVALUATION

While variations in performance review systems are limitless, most of them incorporate the following:

1. A formal job description, usually prepared by staff people.

2. The assignment by the leader of tasks for subordinates, supervision of the day-by-day performance of those tasks, and recognition for good performance and criticism of poor performance on those tasks.

3. A periodic formal evaluation of each subordinate's performance, using some kind of standardized rating form (fitness report, performance review form, employee rating form, merit rating form, etc.).

4. A formal conference or session between the leader and the subordinate in which the leader informs the subordinate what ratings have been given, the reasons for them, and possible ways the subordinate can improve them.

5. Subsequent use of the rating form by others in the organization as a basis for making decisions about subordinates' salaries or wages, promotions, training, etc.

6. Some training of line supervisors in how to do a more objective job of rating subordinates, how to use the form to motivate, etc.

In over 25 years of consulting with many kinds of organizations, I have never seen a performance evaluation system that people liked—either leaders who administer it or subordinates on whom it is used. Typically, performance evaluation causes problems and headaches for both the evaluator and the person evaluated. Being evaluated by another is so often threatening. People dread being told they haven't done a good job or their work is not satisfactory or they're only 4 on a scale of 7. Supervisors, too, dislike sending such messages—they know how they hurt, how they lower a person's self-esteem, how they provoke arguments.

Here are other serious deficiencies in performance evaluations:

1. Job descriptions are usually not adequate for defining specific functions which a subordinate is expected to perform. People with identical job descriptions often end up doing quite different things. And studies generally have shown substantial differences between leaders and subordinates as to what responsibilities and duties the subordinate is expected to perform.

2. Leaders are required to fill out rating forms that usually contain lists of "traits" and "characteristics," such as cooperativeness, initiative, creativity, thoroughness, etc., that are next to impossible to evaluate objectively and accurately.

3. Extreme variations exist in the standards and the rating practices of different leaders. Each has biases and pet ideas about what

ratings should be given ("Nobody gets an Excellent rating from me"; "I never rate anyone Below Average because if he's that bad I shouldn't keep him").

4. Leaders' ratings have a tendency to show the "halo effect": they first make an overall judgment of a subordinate's performance and then indiscriminately rate all specific items consistent with the general rating.

5. Leaders' ratings are strongly influenced by whatever administrative actions they may have to take in the future. ("If I rate too high, she'll expect to get a raise"; "If I rate too high I'll not be able to justify firing her in the future").

6. Ratings of subordinates often cause the same kinds of reactions as the grading of children in school—apple-polishing, covering up, "working only for the grade," competitiveness, arguments, loss of self-esteem, etc.

7. Most performance evaluation systems focus only on past performance—they look back on what has already happened rather than encourage effective performance in the future.

8. While leaders are supposed to explain and discuss subordinates' evaluations with them, some avoid these conferences like the plague. They know they'll be unpleasant.

Improvements in performance evaluation are long overdue. What is needed is a system that incorporates all that is known about human motivation and needs, as well as being consistent with our concept of leader effectiveness. More specifically, a system needs to be designed to:

1. Make work a more meaningful and need-fulfilling experience.

2. Demonstrate to employees that their ideas and contributions are valued and needed.

3. Provide guidance for people to grow and develop so they can experience the satisfaction of being more competent today than they were yesterday.

4. Increase people's feeling of freedom and self-determination through involvement in improving their own performance.

If these goals are reached, employees will feel that *they are the organization,* and then they will want to contribute to its success.

THE PERIODIC PLANNING CONFERENCE (PPC)

Over several years, I developed for my client organizations a radically new approach to performance appraisal. I am now convinced it is one of the most important tools of an effective leader.

The PPC is a regularly scheduled conference with each of the leader's subordinates, generally every year or six months. The length of the conference may vary from a half hour to two or more hours. Sometimes the conference has to be spread over more than one meeting.

It is a specified time set aside for the supervisor and the subordinate to lay out a plan of what the subordinate intends to do during the next six months to improve performance, to develop new skills, and to institute changes in carrying out functions of the job. The subordinate is also invited to discuss ways for the supervisor to help the subordinate accomplish the next six months' goals.

It is an opportunity for subordinates to discuss with the supervisor *any* problem or concern that may be affecting their job performance, job satisfaction, or future with the company.

Rather than focus on past performance (what already has been done), the PPC requires the supervisor and the subordinates to focus on future performance (what *can* be done). Thereby, the PPC to a great extent eliminates the distasteful feature of most merit-rating systems—namely, the supervisor's having to evaluate, judge, and rate subordinates' past performance.

The PPC requires the subordinate and supervisor to focus on the job, the work, the goals, the programs—all job-related activities. Thus the PPC eliminates another distasteful feature of merit-rating systems: rating personal traits such as loyalty, cooperativeness, conscientiousness, leadership, etc. The PPC does away with "scores," which in most merit-rating systems cause so much defensiveness on the part of the subordinates and arguments between the supervisor and the subordinates.

The PPC, unlike most merit-rating systems, is a *two-way* conference. Subordinates participate even more than the supervisor in setting their own goals and planning their own activities. In addition, subordinates are encouraged to suggest how the supervisor can be better at helping them achieve their goals.

The Rationale of the PPC

Underlying the PPC is a set of conceptions about what you should be trying to accomplish with your work group.

First, it is your responsibility to improve the individual's performance in his or her work. By-product benefits from the PPC that will also accrue to the company include: identifying qualified reserves for each level of management, providing means for systematic follow-up and development of people, focus on job performance instead of personality traits, helping people to help themselves grow in the job and the organization.

Your next purpose is to build a relationship between yourself and your subordinates that will encourage free discussion concerning job problems so everybody will know where they stand and will be encouraged and confident that whenever job problems arise, something can and will be done about it.

You want to concentrate on the future. True, people do learn from past experience and planning requires data from the past; nevertheless, you should always keep your eye on the future. It will then be unnecessary to "cry over spilled milk." You can avoid the unpleasant aspects of evaluating the past and, instead, concentrate on doing something positive to improve working relationships in the future.

You will get employees more involved in their own work by giving them the freedom to recommend their own performance goals. As we will see, this should increase their interest and enthusiasm in their job because they will be making contributions to meet their own needs and those of the company.

Finally, you will provide the opportunity to resolve conflicts when they arise, in a manner acceptable to both participants. You will also provide guidance in helping each employee plan his or her career and develop and grow as an individual. And you will be building a mutually rewarding relationship between yourself and your subordinates.

Some Assumptions Underlying the PPC

The PPC approach is founded on certain assumptions. It should prove helpful to keep these in mind and to discuss them with your subordinates.

1. Companies must progress in the marketplace or they will be bypassed by their competitors. By the same token, the employees of an enterprise, in general, must change in order to progress. A significant number of them must continue to improve, grow, and develop for the company to move forward. After all, the company is comprised of people and, if the company is to move forward, so must the people who work there. Most people really don't want to stand still. If they cannot expand on their jobs, they will find ways to do it off the job. Learning is fun and people will seek new ways to learn whenever they have the opportunity.

2. There is *always* a better way of doing things. I hope

this assumption can be substituted for the old saying, "We've been doing it that way for years, so why change?" Experience with the PPC has proven that each time subordinates review the functions and goals of their positions, they do a better job of stating them, measuring them, and achieving them.

3. No one is *ever* working at 100 percent capacity. Perhaps no one can—but the evidence indicates that most people, even those who are effective, are only working at a fraction of their true capacity.

4. Change, growth, and modification are inevitable characteristics of an effective organization.

5. People are not strongly motivated to accomplish goals set by others. Someone has stated this amusingly as, "No one is apathetic except in pursuit of someone else's goals." In fact, how often have we all seen resistance generated by commands and orders passed down from higher-ups? We see the same resistance from children in the home and from students in schools. It has almost become a way of life in America to resist authority. How much more interesting life would be if all of us could be more in charge of our jobs! How often have you said to yourself, "I'll do what the boss says but nobody knows my job as well as I do, and I can do it better if he would let me alone"?

6. People work hard to accomplish goals they set for themselves. But they experience this opportunity so rarely that you can expect a burst of enthusiasm when they are given a chance. People get sick of having someone else set goals for them, not because they resent authority, but because they have talent that is not being used. They want to exercise their muscles. There may be some exceptions—some subordinates will be frightened of the prospect of setting their own goals; others may be suspicious of your motives. To cope with these possibili-

ties, it is very important that you use your Active Listening skills and Method III.

7. People are happier when given a chance to accomplish more. A sense of accomplishment, the feeling that they have done something worthwhile, brings most people pleasure and a sense of importance. The more often they can experience these satisfying feelings, the more interested and enthusiastic they will become and the more they will attempt to repeat the experience. The challenge to you as a supervisor is to see how frequently you can give subordinates such opportunities.

HOW TO PREPARE FOR THE PPC

Preparation for the PPC requires several discrete steps. I'll describe each of these in detail:

STEP I: Preparing Your People

Leaders who want to introduce the PPC in their own work group should remember that any new idea or new system usually encounters resistance to change. So they must take steps to reduce this effect and to deal with subordinates' feelings.

1. Explain the deficiencies of traditional performance-rating systems.

2. Explain the rationale of the PPC and the assumptions underlying it.

3. Listen to the feelings of your subordinates.

4. Get them willing to try the new PPC system on an experimental basis.

In some organizations, leaders may be able to get management approval to substitute the PPC system for the traditional merit-rating system. In other organizations this may not be possible for various reasons. *Any leader can still introduce the PPC as a system to be used on top of (or in addition to) the formal merit-rating system.* This means that you can work within the traditional rating system and at the same time use a second system that is much more likely to achieve the goals of higher productivity, higher morale, greater independence of subordinates, greater respect for subordinates, and greater motivation of subordinates.

STEP II. Getting Mutual Agreement on Job Functions

It is very important for both the leader and the subordinate to reach a Method III agreement on what functions the subordinate is expected to carry out on his job. Problems and conflicts arise when there are differences between the two.

In preparing for the initial PPC it is therefore important to obtain mutual agreement between the leader and each subordinate on "job functions."

"Job functions" are not "duties," nor are they what is usually included in a job description or position description.

A job function is more like a description of a subordinate's *contribution to the organization*—what he does for the organization to warrant being paid a salary or wage. To illustrate, contrast the traditional "list of duties" of a personnel director with her "job functions."

Duties	Job Functions
Recruit, interview, and screen applicants for jobs.	Fill job openings as requested by department heads with qualified people within an established time period and cost standard.

Conduct surveys of employee morale.	Be aware of employee problems or dissatisfactions early enough to assist department heads in the resolution of such problems.
Administer workmen's compensation program.	Process claims for compensation within a standard time period and cost standard.

Here are questions you can use with your subordinates to help them understand what you mean when you say you want a list of job functions:

1. What do you do to contribute to the organization?

2. What do you do that warrants the organization paying you a salary?

3. Why does your job exist? What is it supposed to contribute?

4. When you feel you are doing a good job, what are you actually accomplishing for the organization?

Here is a sample list of job functions developed for a secretary's job:

1. Answer all incoming telephone calls and greet visitors in a way that will give a favorable impression of the department.

2. Provide services requested in incoming telephone calls independently of the boss whenever possible.

3. Transcribe and edit boss's letters accurately and quickly.

4. Maintain boss's schedule of appointments so it is always up to date and accurate.

5. Develop and maintain a filing system that permits quick access to all previous correspondence.

6. Maintain an inventory of office supplies and initiate purchase requests early enough to maintain a ready supply.

7. Answer routine administrative correspondence independently.

Here is the procedure recommended for obtaining a list of mutually agreed-upon job functions:

1. Explain carefully the definition of "job function" as opposed to "duty."

2. Ask the subordinate to develop a list. If several subordinates have identical jobs, you can ask them to do this as a group.

3. As the leader, develop your own list of the subordinate's functions.

After your subordinate has prepared his or her own list of job functions, you will be ready to review them together. Remember that the subordinate has the "ball"— let him or her carry the discussion. You might give him or her a choice of going through each function one by one until they have all been covered and then go back and review them later; or you might agree on meaning and wording, one by one, until the entire list has been covered. It doesn't really make any difference which method you use as long as you both agree on the meaning of each function.

It is not crucial that the list of functions exactly follows the format I have outlined or that it is unclear to other people. As long as you and the subordinate understand what each function means, you are well on your way to achieving your objective. Naturally, it is best that everything be as clear as possible.

STEP III: Getting Mutual Agreement on How Performance Is to Be Measured

Once a list of job functions is developed, the next step is to get mutual agreement between the leader and subordinate on how performance on each of the job functions will be *measured*.

This step has two purposes: (1) to reduce misunderstandings between the leader and subordinate, and (2) to point up what data the subordinate will need to evaluate his or her own performance.

What are "Measures" of Performance?

Leaders are constantly using different measures of a subordinate's performance. When a leader evaluates a secretary by such statements as "She types a very accurate letter" or "She is marvelous at handling phone calls," he certainly has *in his mind* some measure of those two job functions. The problem is that the measures too often remain in the mind of the leader. They never get transmitted to the subordinate.

What is needed is a way of getting the subordinate to understand (and agree with) the measures to be used in evaluating performance in each of the job functions.

What is a "measure" of performance? In the case of the secretary's accurate letters, the boss's measure might be the *number of errors in spelling and punctuation.*

Measures tell us *how* another's performance is evaluated; they do not tell us whether the performance is good or bad. We measure a person's height by number of inches. But the measure does not tell anyone how tall a particular person is. We measure long distances by number of miles, but that phrase says nothing about how far you drove that day.

How to Get Mutually Accepted Measures

1. Ask your subordinate to take the list of job functions and develop measures for each of the functions. Coach him or her by asking:

   "How do you know when you feel you're doing a good job or a poor one when performing that function?"

   "What measures do *you* have in your mind?"

"What data or facts are you looking at when you're performing well? Or poorly?"

2. Encourage the subordinate to develop *quantitative* measures whenever possible, but remember, for certain functions precise quantitative measures may not be available. Here are examples of quantitative and "subjective" (nonquantitative) measures:

Quantitative Measures	*Subjective Measures*
Number of errors	Neatness of appearance
Number of rejects	Politeness on the telephone
Number of complaints	Satisfaction of customers
Dollar sales volume	Pleasantness of manner
Dollar net profit	Creativity, innovativeness
Dollar cost reduction	
Number of items produced	
Number of deadlines met	
Number of new customers	
Number of people trained	
Scores on achievement tests	

3. Develop your own measures for each of the subordinate's job functions.

4. Get together and compare your measures. Then discuss, evaluate, modify. End up with mutually accepted measures for each of the subordinate's job functions.

IMPORTANT POINT: Once Steps I, II, and III (in preparing for the PPC) have been accomplished with each of your subordinates, they need not be repeated, unless later there is some significant change in the job functions of a subordinate.

CONDUCTING THE PPC

Again: adequate preparation for the actual PPC on the part of supervisor and subordinate is essential. It ensures that each of you goes into the conference with clear ideas of what is required for the next six months. The conference then becomes a matching process: *your* goals and programs are matched with the goals and programs of the *subordinate*. Stated in a different way, the PPC becomes a *two-way problem-solving conference* in which supervisor and subordinate work out a *mutually acceptable plan* for the subordinate. Then you discuss ways for you to help the subordinate accomplish this plan. To set the stage:

1. Set the date for the PPC in advance, preferably at least one week.

2. At that time ask your subordinate to prepare his or her goals in preparation for the conference.

3. Provide an opportunity to ask questions about the PPC.

4. Explain that the focus of the PPC will be on the future, not the past —and that you expect the subordinate to "carry the ball" in presenting his or her list of goals.

5. Explain your own goals for your work group, so the subordinate knows exactly what your own overall performance goals are for the next period.

You may wish to use some of the following questions to help subordinates begin to think about goals:

"What do you want to accomplish in the coming year?"

"In which of your job functions do you feel the need for improvement?"

"What are your goals for doing a more effective job?"

"What is your program this year for improving your performance or the performance of your work group?"

If these preliminaries to the conference have been carried out, the actual PPC should take care of itself, providing you allow the subordinate to have primary control of the conference.

This does not mean you play a passive role. Certainly,

you'll want to make sure that the subordinate's goals and plans for improvement are sufficient to accomplish your aims. For example, if during the conference it becomes clear that a particular subordinate has not set up a goal to improve his or her performance, say, in cost reduction, and yet your goal is to get costs reduced, then obviously you must suggest the inclusion of a cost reduction goal in his or her plan. Similarly, if you feel that some goal set by another subordinate is unrealistic and not likely to be achieved for whatever reason, you may want to suggest that he or she lower the standard somewhat.

Here are key points to remember:

1. It is the subordinate's ball. Get his or her ideas and feelings out first. Active Listen.

2. Remember to keep the discussion forward looking—the past is gone.

3. When it's your turn to talk, be candid, honest, and open. Send I-messages.

4. Secure agreement on the goals to be accomplished. Keep their number to a workable size. Use Method III.

5. As a supervisor you will want to have a clear understanding of how your subordinate plans to reach each goal—what actions are planned.

6. Whenever you feel there is an opportunity or a need, you can certainly share ideas with the subordinate on how to reach the goals. It is this sharing of ideas that makes the PPC a meaningful, worthwhile experience.

7. Maintain a climate that is warm, friendly, and informal, yet task-oriented. Remember, this is your associate, and you need his or her help to attain your goals.

8. Remember, setting goals is making a commitment to change. So, some subordinates might resist sticking their necks out.

9. Review and put in writing the goals agreed upon, with a copy for each of you.

IMPLEMENTING THE DECISIONS MADE IN THE PPC

Important functions have to be performed to help the subordinate reach his or her goals: (1) You may need to provide the subordinate with data he or she needs to evaluate progress; (2) You must provide whatever material, financial, or personnel resources are required; (3) You must make yourself available as a counselor or facilitator of problem-solving, should the subordinate encounter problems.

Providing Your Subordinate the Data for Self-Evaluation

One of the most important purposes of the PPC is to shift primary responsibility for evaluation of the subordinate's performance from the *leader* to the *subordinate*.

The key idea here is TRUST—trust in your subordinates' desire to do their jobs well and to accomplish their goals.

For subordinates to evaluate their own performance continually, they need appropriate data. Exactly *what* data will be determined, of course, by the measures developed in Step III in preparing for the PPC.

If you and a particular subordinate agreed upon "dollar cost reduction" as a measure of his or her performance in one job function, then you must do what is necessary to get those dollar cost figures continually fed to him or her. This may require you to get the accounting department to agree to furnish these figures weekly or monthly.

Providing Subordinate Resources

One way of defining your role following the PPC is to think of yourself as a "first assistant" to your subordinates, assisting them in whatever ways are necessary to help them reach their goals. This may mean agreeing to supply them with additional funds, additional materials, or additional personnel. Failure to follow through on these commitments will certainly hurt your relationships and produce resentment.

Facilitating Problem-Solving

Inevitably, subordinates will encounter problems as they try to accomplish their goals. It is the function of the leader to help when such problems come up. Remember, facilitating problem-solving is what a leader is for, as pointed out in Chapter III.

You will need Active Listening in such sessions to help keep responsibility with the subordinate for solving a problem. Encourage the subordinate to go through the "Six Steps of the Problem-Solving Process." You might even write these steps on a blackboard or chart pad:

STEP I: What is the problem?

STEP II: What are possible solutions?

STEP III: How do you evaluate these solutions?

STEP IV: Which solution seems best?

STEP V: *Who* needs to do *what* by *when*?

STEP VI: How will you evaluate the outcome?

You should also feel free to initiate a problem-solving session if you begin to see a problem that might interfere with the subordinate's reaching a particular goal. Again, your attitude should be "What can I do to help?", not "You're failing here—what's wrong?"

Expected Benefits from the PPC

Whether the PPC *replaces* or *supplements* the traditional performance review or merit-rating system in your organization, you can expect certain outcomes from this new approach.

First, you will find that your subordinates will respond to your trust by becoming more responsible and less dependent on you.

Second, you can expect higher motivation from your subordinates. It will be *their* goals they will be trying to reach, not goals imposed on them by their supervisor.

Third, their job will bring them more self-fulfillment and satisfaction.

Fourth, you'll find yourself spending less time supervising and overseeing them.

Fifth, you can expect continuous improvement in your subordinates' performance. Doing things better will become the accepted norm in your work unit.

Don't expect, however, that the new PPC program will be carried out without a hitch. It will require modifications from time to time. Some subordinates will find it hard at first to give up being dependent and to stop "doing only what they're told to do." Measures of job functions may need revision, or you may find it difficult to get the right data.

As with anything new, adjustments will be required. Yet once the bugs are worked out, the Periodic Planning Conference will bring tangible rewards to your subordinates, to yourself, and to the organization.

XII. SOME DEEPER ISSUES FOR LEADERS

LEADERS must choose the kind of leader they want to be, and nobody else can make that choice for them. How do you choose from among alternative styles of leadership?

Naturally, in making your choice you will first want to consider the criterion of *effectiveness* (the central emphasis throughout this book). What leadership style will make you more effective—in building a team, making good decisions, getting productivity, fostering morale, and so on? You may also want to ask yourself other questions to help you focus on equally important issues:

What kind of person do you want to be?

What kind of relationships do you want?

What kind of organization do you want?

What kind of society do you want?

WHAT KIND OF PERSON DO YOU WANT TO BE?

The style of leadership you choose will greatly influence the kind of person you will become. You'll not be able to separate the two. Because you spend a lot of your time in your role as leader, how you behave in that role will inexorably shape you as a person.

To illustrate, a leadership style that depends heavily on coercive power will require you to maintain a rather consistent attitude of suspicion and distrust. You'll have to be guarded in what you tell people, be on guard to detect signs of resistance to your power (or outright insubordination). Along with this vigilance, as an authoritarian leader you will find yourself viewing others as possessing limited capacity and low potential for self-direction, for constructive change and personal development, for thinking for themselves.

If you choose coercive power as your way of leadership, it will make an impact on your personal life in other ways. As I pointed out earlier, by assuming all the responsibility for group decisions and taking on the total burden for implementing and enforcing policies and rules you will pay a price of increased tension, worry, and anxiety—and ultimately have poorer physical and mental health.

Another issue: do you want to be a person who is open, honest, and direct in dealing with others? Psychologists use the term "congruence" to refer to the similarity between what a person is thinking or feeling *inside* and what he or she communicates to the *outside*. Do you want to say what you mean and mean what you say, or be a person who "doesn't ring true" and can't be trusted by others? Do you want to be a person who sends honest and direct I-messages to let people know exactly where you stand?

There is, almost needless to say, a risk in being congruent in your communications, and you should seriously consider whether you can take that risk. If you decide to be a leader who is open, honest, and direct in *presenting yourself as you really are,* you risk exposing your true self to others. An I-message sender is "transparently real"—to self and others. People must have courage to *be* what they are—that is, to communicate what they feel and think as of each moment in their lives. And here is the risk: if you open yourself to others, they will get to know the real you! Do you want people to know how you really are?

If you decide to be a leader who listens to others, there is another risk. Active Listening, as you have seen, requires you temporarily to suspend your own thoughts, feelings, evaluations, and judgments in order to attend exclusively to the message of the sender. It *forces* accurate receiving. For, if you are to understand the message in terms of the sender's meaning, you must put yourself into the shoes of the sender (into his frame of reference, into his world of reality). Only then can you hear the meaning *intended* by the sender. The "feedback" part of Active Listening is nothing more than your ultimate check on the accuracy of your listening, although it also assures the sender that you have understood.

Active Listening carries its own risk. Something happens to a person who practices Active Listening. When you understand accurately how another person thinks or feels, put yourself momentarily into the other person's shoes, see the world as another is seeing it—you run the risk of having your own opinions and attitudes changed.

People do get changed by what they *really understand.* To be "open to the experience" of another invites having to reinterpret your own. People who cannot listen to others are "defensive" because they cannot afford to expose themselves to ideas and views different from their own.

In summary, effective two-way communication, requiring both *congruence* (clear sending) and *Active Listening* (accurate receiving), entails two risks: the exposure of the way we really *are* and the possibility of *becoming* different. This is why effective interpersonal communication requires inner security and personal courage.

Are you willing to become this kind of person? Can you

find the inner security and the personal courage you'll need for open, honest, direct two-way communication with others?

WHAT KIND OF RELATIONSHIPS DO YOU WANT?

The kind of leader you are will strongly influence, if not determine, what kind of relationships you will have with the people in your group and in the organization. Considering how much time you spend with these people, this obviously is a matter of importance in choosing your leadership style.

At many points throughout this book I have referred to the impact of power-based authoritarian leadership on the relationship between leaders and group members: how power reduces communication from group members to the leader; how power builds status barriers between leaders and their subordinates, thus reducing member-initiated interactions; how members cover up their problems and lie about their mistakes; how power generates hostility and resentment; how power, to be effective, requires that people be afraid and dependent; and how power-wielding leaders must guard against getting "buddy-buddy" with subordinates.

I've not yet mentioned another logical consequence of your being an authoritarian leader—quite simply, you'll have much less *fun* than leaders who don't depend on power. By fun, I am thinking of many things: laughing with others at your own mistakes and limitations, and at theirs; joining with others to tackle a sticky problem and being rewarded with a surprisingly creative solution; becoming close friends with some of your subordinates; sharing your failures openly and without fear of destructive evaluation; watching people grow and develop in their job; relating to others as persons, not as mere positions in the organization. These pleasant things happen in groups and organizations where relationships are more equalitarian, devoid of fear and resentment.

Do you want helping relationships with people or manipulative and exploitative ones? The benefits of helping relationships are substantial: seeing people solve their own problems and become less dependent; watching people become more open in discussing their problems; experiencing the personal satisfaction of helping people get their needs met. And, as I pointed out earlier, when you help others meet their needs, they are infinitely more willing to make an effort to help you meet yours. This reciprocal quality invariably develops in relationships when coercive power is eschewed.

Several years ago I attempted to describe in writing, as succinctly as I could, the basic philosophy underlying my idea of the effective parent-child relationship. It later was incorporated in all the other human relations courses we developed, so it has become a general philosophy for all effective human relationships—parent-child, teacher-student, husband-wife, leader-group member, and so on. My description was a declaration of intent—a statement of the kind of relationship anyone might want to foster with another. It is called "A Credo for My Relationships."

Each person who completes one of our courses gets a copy of the Credo, but I also receive many requests from others. Some people have it framed or decoupaged for hanging on a wall; others have had it reprinted and sent as a Christmas card. A few people included the reading of the Credo in their wedding ceremony as a public affirmation of the philosophy they wanted to live by in their marriage. My own daughter, Judy, asked me to read the Credo at her wedding to John Sands.

The Credo obviously has had a great deal of meaning to a lot of people. It seems to represent, in plain terms, what a lot of people are striving for in their human relationships. In it you will recognize most of the essential elements of my concept of leader effectiveness.

A CREDO

For My Relationships

You and I are in a relationship which I value and want to keep. Yet each of us is a separate person with unique needs and the right to meet those needs.

When you are having problems meeting your needs, I will try to listen with genuine acceptance, in order to facilitate your finding your own solutions instead of depending on mine. I also will try to respect your right to choose your own beliefs and develop your own values, different though they may be from mine.

However, when your behavior interferes with what I must do to get my own needs met, I will tell you openly and honestly how your behavior affects me, trusting that you respect my needs and feelings enough to try to change the behavior that is unacceptable to me. Also, whenever some behavior of mine is unacceptable to you, I hope you will tell me openly and honestly so I can try to change my behavior.

At those times when we find that either of us cannot change to meet the other's needs, let us acknowledge that we have a conflict and commit ourselves to resolve each such conflict without either of us resorting to the use of power or authority to win at the expense of the other's losing. I respect your needs, but I also must respect my own. So let us always strive to search for a solution that will be acceptable to both of us. Your needs will be met, and so will mine—neither will lose, both will win.

In this way, you can continue to develop as a person through satisfying your needs, and so can I. Thus, ours can be a healthy relationship in which both of us can strive to become what we are capable of being. And we can continue to relate to each other with mutual respect, love, and peace.

WHAT KIND OF ORGANIZATION DO YOU WANT?

In choosing a leadership style, leaders cannot avoid facing another issue: what kind of organizations are we to have in our society? Organizations, after all, are made up of people whose leadership style will determine the psychological climate of the total organization. Repressive leaders make repressive organizations.

What kind of leadership style is required so all members of the organization feel their needs are respected? It is inconsistent with the philosophy of leadership advocated in this book that an organization exists solely for the realization of the needs and goals of its leaders. So leaders must find ways to enlist the participation of group members in making decisions that will result in mutual need satisfaction of management and employees, leaders and group members.

Do you want to be in an organization that is flexible enough to adapt to changing conditions? If organizations are going to survive and prosper they must have this flexibility. Problems should not be solved nor decisions made on the time-honored basis of who has the most authority, but rather on the basis of the creative resources of all members who have data relevant to the problem.

Organizations will have difficulty surviving if they rely exclusively on management methods based on workers' fear of losing their jobs or being deprived of their basic needs. That is why in the last decade or two we have witnessed the start of a revolution—call it the human relations revolution. Millions of dollars are being spent by organizations in the search for new patterns of supervision, new management practices, new styles of leadership. It may be that to survive in a democratic society, organizations must discover ways of operating democratically. James Worthy, then an industrial relations executive with Sears, Roebuck, expressed this same idea persuasively some years ago:

> If we are concerned with the preservation of "free enterprise" in America and freedom in the world, we must strengthen its principles more effectively to the internal organization and administration of our own business. . . . First of all, the system must continue to work effectively. It cannot do that for long unless it does a better job of tapping the creative resources, ability, and productivity of its individual members.

The leadership philosophy and methods described in this book seem singularly right for reaching Worthy's objective.

WHAT KIND OF SOCIETY DO YOU WANT?

Although, in theory, our society is deeply rooted in the belief that all citizens have the right (and the capacity) to select their goals and make critical decisions, most of our social institutions tend to reserve this right for the leaders of those organizations. It is apparent that democracy *in practice* is not always the same as democracy *in theory*.

Freedom from dependence is yet another criterion of a democratic society. As James Marshall, the eminent attorney, once wrote:

> Freedom from dependence is the very basis of democracy. It is necessary if [persons] are to develop and utilize their capabilities, if society is to be a balance of their individualities and not a structure of status. Freedom from dependence is requisite to maturity. For the satisfaction achieved through dependence is an uneasy peace in the shadow of some power in which one has little share.

When power is concentrated in (and employed by) only a few leaders, dependence increases. The challenge for our society, then, is to encourage its leaders to embrace a leadership style more consistent with the democratic principles we have learned to cherish—in theory at least. And this conception of leadership will need to be injected into the bloodstream of every organization and institution in our society.

If we want a democratic *society* we must have democratic *organizations*, which in turn will require democratic *leaders* who themselves have the necessary skills and methods to develop mutually satisfying *relationships* with the people they lead.

A Personal Postscript

I began to realize rather early in life, even before I went to high school, that there were good leaders and poor leaders in my world. I was not exactly sure what made the difference, but I remember thinking it had something to do with how much those people used their power—how much they punished or threatened to punish, how much they ordered me around, how much they tried to control me. These leaders were my various teachers, two school principals, a YMCA leader, two coaches, a Boy Scout leader, several camp counselors, a number of Sunday school teachers, my minister, and a mean assistant principal I shall never forget.

It was also very clear that with those I felt were "good" leaders I behaved one way and with the "poor" leaders quite another way. I liked myself much better with the good ones, and naturally I liked them. I worked harder at whatever activities the group was involved in, and I usually had a lot of fun. It was also easy to talk to these adults, and with them I enjoyed a kind of mutual kidding relationship.

With the poor ones, I always took on a different role and behaved in ways I didn't like at all. I was not a productive member of the group; I spent a lot of time figuring out how to get back at these leaders by embarrassing them or putting them down; I resisted their direction; I acted the clown for the other group members; I often lied or covered up my mistakes; and I seldom had conversations or jokes with them. I didn't like me in these relationships, and I certainly didn't like them.

While all this puzzled me, I'm sure I didn't think very deeply or analytically about leaders and leadership until I myself became a leader of a group of ten or more officers in the Army Air Corps during World War II. While I was highly motivated to be one of those "good" leaders, I soon discovered it wasn't that easy. When I pushed my group too hard, I got rebellion and resistance. I didn't want to threaten punishment for poor performance, yet rewards never worked for me either. Several of the members who had been my friends stopped being so friendly. Alliances often were formed against my well-conceived policies.

Soon I became much more analytical about leadership. How does one get good performance from a group? How can leaders maintain good relationships with those over whom they are responsible? How does one develop a cohesive group with "team spirit"?

Several years after returning to civilian life, I was invited to spend the summer of 1949 on a project at the National Training Laboratory for Group Development. Understandably, I saw this as a great opportunity to learn more about groups and leaders, especially since NTL (as it later was called) was a new leadership training center run by a group of pioneer scholars in this relatively new field.

That summer's experience marked the beginning of my professional interest in leadership, an interest that I have never lost. I soon became a "leadership trainer," read everything I could find on groups and leadership, and eventually developed what I thought was a rather coherent and promising new theory of effective leadership, which I published in a book—my first—called *Group Centered Leadership: A Way of Releasing the Creative Potential of Groups* (Boston: Houghton Mifflin, 1955). As it turned out, however, my colleagues in the field did not judge my model of effective leadership the same way I did. In fact, I am certain most of them didn't even read the book. And seldom were my ideas referred to in publications on leadership.

Either it was a bad book or an inadequate model, or, as I now prefer to believe, it was too "radical" for its time. I was advocating some ideas that ran contrary to much of the thinking at that time—that leaders should never use their power, that they should involve group members in making all important decisions, that groups exist to meet the needs of all their members, that leaders can trust the "wisdom of the group," that group members should participate in setting the group goals, that leaders should try to reduce the status differential between them and their group members, that rewards and punishment are ineffective as motivators, that leaders should learn the skills of the professional counselor.

Today, as professionals in the field know, these notions are in the mainstream of thinking about organizational leadership, and many have been verified by research studies. This is not to say that my earlier model contained everything that social scientists now know about effective leadership. Quite the contrary. Much more has been added to the body of knowledge about the complex relationship between leaders and followers; advances have been made in our understanding of group behavior and group development, what motivates group members, and what fosters creativity and productivity.

I have incorporated these additions and refinements

in this book, as well as drawn heavily from my twenty years' experience consulting with many different kinds of organizations. And, not to be overlooked, my present conception of leader effectiveness has been shaped and polished by a decade of training thousands of managers and administrators in my Leader Effectiveness Training (L.E.T.) course. This 36-hour course is made available to organizations through a nationwide network of several hundred instructors who have been trained and certified to teach it.

For their significant contributions to my thinking, I wish to acknowledge and thank certain persons.

I am indebted to my teacher, colleague, and friend, Carl Rogers, who helped me appreciate the creative capacity that resides in every individual for solving problems and the listening skills for releasing those capacities.

Frederick Llewellyn, General Manager of Forest Lawn Memorial Park, in Los Angeles, California, showed his faith in me for fifteen years by giving me the opportunity to test out all my ideas, in every division and at every level of his organization, then consisting of around a thousand employees.

Ralph Jones, now Director of Training for my organization, Effectiveness Training, Inc., made valuable contributions to the content and methodology of the L.E.T. course, as have several other L.E.T. instructors.

Recently, I discovered a little-known book by T. O. Jacobs—*Leadership and Exchange in Formal Organizations* (Alexandria, Virginia: Human Resources Research Organization, 1971)—in which he provides what, in my opinion, is the most insightful and lucid synthesis of the findings from the thousands of research studies on leadership, creatively utilizing the "social exchange theory" as his integrating vehicle. I wish to acknowledge how much his thinking helped clear up some of my own.

I also wish to thank those L.E.T. instructors who contibuted case material and examples, many of which I used in this book. And I am grateful to Karen Gleason, who found time in her busy schedule to type the manuscript.

Finally, I would be less than candid if I failed to state my own strong bias that a high level of effectiveness with the skills mentioned in this book seldom is acquired without extensive L.E.T. classroom training. I would be glad to provide details on this classroom program and the process my firm uses to train and authorize qualified trainers to teach L.E.T. Please direct your inquiries to:

L.E.T. Information
Effectiveness Training, Inc.
531 Stevens Avenue
Solana Beach, California 92075
Call 800-628-1197 for more information.

TECHNICAL APPENDIX

For the benefit of scientifically oriented readers, these pages provide references for the various studies and findings cited throughout the book.

CHAPTER I

Page 1. The recently published survey and review of leadership research is: Stogdill, Ralph M. *Handbook of Leadership.* New York: Free Press, 1974.

Pages 4–6. The study of an industrial leader is described in the author's first book, now out of print. Gordon, Thomas. *Group-Centered Leadership.* The investigation was conducted by Robert Burns, then Director of the Industrial Relations Center, University of Chicago.

Page 8. From Leonard Woodcock's introduction to Gyllenhammar, Pehr G. *People at Work.* Reading, Mass: Addison-Wesley Publishing Co., 1977.

CHAPTER II

Page 14. The concept of the "inner child of the past" is taken from Missildine, W. Hugh. *Your Inner Child of the Past.* New York: Simon and Schuster, 1963.

Page 15. The list of coping mechanisms is more completely described in Gordon, Thomas. *P.E.T.: Parent Effectiveness Training.* New York: Wyden Books, 1970.

Page 17. My outline of how leaders acquire followers was strongly influenced by Knickerbocker, Irving. Leadership: a conception and some implications. *Journal of Social Issues,* 1948, 4, 23–40.

Page 20. The two sets of leadership skills were drawn from Bowers, D. G., and Seashore, S. E. Predicting organizational effectiveness with a four-factor theory of leadership. *Administrative Science Quarterly,* 11, 1966, 238–263.

Page 20. That the effective leader must be both a "human relations specialist" and a "productivity specialist" is derived from Moment, David, and Zaleznik, Abraham. *Role Development and Interpersonal Competence.* Cambridge, Mass.: Harvard University Press, 1963.

Page 22. From Maslow, A. H. A theory of human motivation. *Psychological Review,* 50, 1943, 370–396.

Page 24. Herzberg's two-factor theory of motivation is from Herzberg, F., Mausner, B., and Snyderman, B. A. *The Motivation to Work.* New York: John Wiley & Sons, 1959.

Page 26. The Texas Instruments findings were reported in Myers, M. Scott. Who are your motivated workers? *Harvard Business Review,* 42, 1964, 73–88.

Page 27. Evidence that effective leaders are good at problem-solving is shown in a study by Greer, F. L. Leader indulgence and group performance. *Psychological Monographs,* 75, 1961, 1–33.

CHAPTER III

Page 37. The idea of groups having a definition of "fair exchange" is derived from Jacobs, T. O. *Leadership and Exchange in Formal Organizations.* Human Resources Research Organization, Alexandria, Va. 1971.

Page 39. Paluev, K. K. How collective genius contributes to industrial progress. *General Electric Review,* May, 1941, 254–261.

Page 39. Marrow, Alfred, Bowers, D. G., and Seashore, S. E. *Management by Participation.* New York: Harper & Row, 1968.

Page 42. The "linking pin" function is derived from Likert, Rensis. *New Patterns of Management.* New York: McGraw-Hill, 1961.

Page 43. From a study by Blau, Peter M. *Exchange and Power in Social Life.* New York: John Wiley & Sons, 1964.

CHAPTER IV

Page 56. The term "Active Listening" was first suggested to me by Richard Farson. However, the technique itself is derived from the work of Carl Rogers and his psychology students, then at Ohio State University. At that time it was labeled "reflection of feelings."

Page 63. For a more detailed analysis of the many inhibiting effects of the Roadblocks, see Gordon, Thomas. *P.E.T.: Parent Effectiveness Training.* New York: Wyden Books, 1970.

CHAPTER VI

Pages 97–98. Experimental evidence for the ineffectiveness of You-messages is contained in a Survey Research Center study that showed that foremen of *low-producing* work groups tended to react more punitively

TECHNICAL APPENDIX **273**

and emotionally to failure in performance of their subordinates than foremen of *high-producing* work groups. See Likert, *op. cit.*

Page 104. The concept of the "changee in the driver's seat" comes from Leavitt, Harold J. *Managerial Psychology.* Chicago: University of Chicago Press, 1958.

CHAPTER VII

Page 126. The "Model II" leadership approach is derived from Argyris, Chris. *Increasing Leadership Effectiveness.* New York: John Wiley & Sons, 1976.

CHAPTER VIII

Pages 146–147. For the concepts of "preventive" and "self-disclosure" I-messages, I am indebted to Linda Adams, Director of Women's Programs for my organization.

Page 159. For evidence of the effects of a power differential on both frequency and accuracy of upward communication, see the review of studies on this phenomenon in Jacobs, T. O. *Leadership and Exchange in Formal Organizations, op. cit.,* pp. 218–223.

Page 160. Evidence for ingratiating responses to power is found in the study by Jones, E. E., Gergen, K. J., and Jones, R. G. Tactics of ingratiation among leaders and subordinates in a status hierarchy. *Psychological Monographs,* 77, 1963, 1–20.

Page 163. For evidence of defiance and retaliation occurring when power is used, see the study by Brown, Bert. The effects of need to maintain face on interpersonal bargaining. *Journal of Experimental Social Psychology,* 4, 1968, 107–122.

Page 164. The tendency of individuals of lesser power to form coalitions is illustrated in the study by Vinacke, W. E., and Arkoff, A. An experimental study of coalitions in the triad. *American Sociological Review,* 22, 1957, 406–414.

CHAPTER IX

Page 174. The study on family violence was reported by Gelles, R. J., Strauss, M. A., and Steinmetz, S. K. at the 1977 meeting of the American Association for the Advancement of Science.

Page 191. Evidence of higher-quality decisions from Method III is found in Solem, A. R. The influence of the discussion leader's attitude on the outcome of group decisions. Ph.D. dissertation, University of Michigan, 1953.

Page 205. The research showing that effective leaders are strong advocates is reported in Likert, *op. cit.*

Page 210. Evidence that group members are less satisfied with their leader's using group decision-making *when problems are not urgent* comes from a study by Berkowitz, L. Sharing leadership in small decision-making groups. *Journal of Abnormal and Social Psychology,* 48, 1953, 231–238.

CHAPTER XII

Page 263. Some of the ideas about the need for democratic leadership in a democratic society were taken from an earlier book by the author: Gordon, Thomas. *Group-centered Leadership.* Boston: Houghton-Mifflin, 1955.

INDEX